To Cheryl

Keep laughing...
It makes strangers
nervous!

All the best

[signature]

I May Be Big But I Didn't Cause That Solar Eclipse

By
Gordon Kirkland

Bloomington, IN  Milton Keynes, UK

AuthorHouse™
1663 Liberty Drive, Suite 200
Bloomington, IN 47403
www.authorhouse.com
Phone: 1-800-839-8640

AuthorHouse™ UK Ltd.
500 Avebury Boulevard
Central Milton Keynes, MK9 2BE
www.authorhouse.co.uk
Phone: 08001974150

© *2007 Gordon Kirkland. All rights reserved.*

No part of this book may be reproduced, stored in a retrieval system, or transmitted by any means without the written permission of the author.

First published by AuthorHouse 4/10/2007

ISBN: 978-1-4343-0946-4 (sc)

Library of Congress Control Number: 2007902747

Printed in the United States of America
Bloomington, Indiana

This book is printed on acid-free paper.

For Diane, who has put up with me in "thickness and in health" for over 30 years.

Also By Gordon Kirkland

Books

Justice Is Blind – And Her Dog Just Peed In My Cornflakes (winner of the 2000 Stephen Leacock Award of Merit For Humour)

Never Stand Behind A Loaded Horse (winner of the 2005 Stephen Leacock Award of Merit For Humour)

When My Mind Wanders It Brings Back Souvenirs (winner of the 2006 Stephen Leacock Award of Merit For Humour)

I Think I'm Having One Of Those Decades

The Writer's Address Book

Compact Disks

Comedy

I'm Big For My Age

Audiobooks

Never Stand Behind A Loaded Horse – Live

Table of Contents

Acknowledgements xiii
Introduction: I May Be Big,
But I Didn't Cause That Solar Eclipse xv

Friends, Family, Citizens, and Other Forms Of Wildlife 1
   The Future Came. I Expected
   There'd Be Oatmeal Cookies 3
   Vegas Is An Alarming Place To Go
   For Rest And Relaxation 5
   Every Generation Has Its Own Good Old Days 7
   I'm Not Wrong, Just Psychically Mistaken 9
   Face It. Husbands Are Irresponsibly Responsible
   For All Domestic Disasters 11
   Never Try To Reason With An Oak 13
   He's Educated To A Degree 15
   Goodness Gracious Great Balls Of Frozen Dust Particles ... 17
   I've Been To Hell And Back 19
   Of Mice And Men… And Mothers 21
   I Am A Romantic Legend In My Own Mind 23
   With A Friend Like That 25

Everyone Needs A Good Movement From Time To Time 27
   I'm Going To Have A Movement 29
   We Don't Really Live Here Anymore 31
   Homing In On The Search Of Home Ideas 33
   Life (And Death) On The Real Estate Roller-Coaster 35
   The Real Estate Roller Coaster Part Deux 37
   I Can Pack A Lot Of Stuff Into A Movement 39

Is It Just Me Or Does This Kind Of Thing
Happen to Other People? 41
   My Christmas Shopping Doesn't Involve Camping 43
   I'm Just A Speed Demon 45
   I Had My Day In Court 47
   You Crank And I'll Grump 49
   I'm Going To Start Hiding During Full Moons 51
   At Least Clothes Hunting Isn't Dangerous 53
   My Internal Alarm Clock Is Stuck On Snooze 55
   I Guess They Just Don't Serve My Kind There 57

I Don't Need To Go Shopping For My Shortcomings 59
Gimme An R... Gimme An A...
Gimme An I... Gimme and N 61
Aiming For A Traveler's Sanctuary 63
When Healthy Eating Isn't 65
Fame Is Going To The Dogs 67
I'm Not Getting Older I'm Getting Distinguished 69
I Try To Avoid Cows In Heat 71
I Have A Point 73
In The Early Morning Purple Rain 75
Singing Or Something Resembling It 77
Dog Days In Home Improvement Store 79
It's Not Raining, It Pouring 81
I'm Losing My Inherited Company Loyalty 83
...And They Want Me As A Member? 85
What Am I Offered For A Slightly Used Self Esteem? 87
Bad Canadian... No Bacon, Beer, Or Donuts For Me 89
I'm Not Qualified To Shop In Big Hardware Stores 91
I Need No Fault Insurance For Stock Crashes 93
Who Dumped All This White Crap On My Sidewalk? 95

Somebody Call A Doctor 97
I Feel Like I'm Fixin' To Die 99
Recovering With Documentaries 101
Reducing My Personal Colossalness 103
You Could Say I'm Unfeeling 105

Remembering My Pasture As I Head To The Future 107
My Wife Can Beat The Forces of 'Evel' 109
I Was A Different Sort Of Bagboy 111
I Just Don't See Eye-To-Eye With Goats 113
Turtle Takes Taste Of Teutonic Teen 115

**Forget The Highway, I Can Get Lost
On The Information Side Street** 117
The Problem Is Somewhere Between My Keyboard
And The Back Of My Chair 119
GPS: The Global Pestering System 121
Just What I Need - A Computer With Nag Version 3.1 123
Like Father, Like Grandson 125

It Must Be True. It Was In The News..............................127
  Three Infidels Walk Into A Bar... 129
  News From The Relationship Front Lines 131
  Animals Are A Danger To Man And Upholstery 133
  You Can't Toss An Eel In England,
  But You Can Go On A Camel......................................135
  Standing Up For Our Aims 137
  That's Really Cold Cash...139
  E-coli My New Best Friend 141
  Bordering On A Traffic Jam......................................143
  Cn U Rd Dis, I Nu U Cud 145
  You Can Take Me Anywhere, You Just Can't Dress Me Up... 147
  And You Thought You Had Trouble
  Keeping Names Straight 149
  Reason #58 For Not Keeping A Sledge Hammer
  In The Bathroom 151

Down The Road Again 153
  Supersized In A Small World.....................................155
  All The Little Airlines Go Cheap, Cheap, Cheap 157
  Oklahoma – It's A Learning Experience.......................159
  Pssst... Wanna Buy A Hot Week 161
  I Have My Own Air Terror 163
  I'm Headed For Dayton And I'm Actually Happy About It .. 165
  My Country 'Tis Of The True North Strong And Free, Eh?... 167

  About The Author..171
  About The Caricature Logo 173

Acknowledgements

As always, there are many people to thank when it comes time to publish a new book.

First and foremost is Diane, the woman who has put up with my nonsense for the past thirty-three years. She is my wife, my best friend, my strongest ally, and my anchor to the real world. Without her at my side, I could never have gotten so far.

My sons, Mike and Brad, grew up in the newspaper column and in the earlier books, something I'm sure was at times, not the easiest thing to do. They have both grown to be strong successful young men. I hope they know just how much they have helped me through the years, even if it does become a topic of conversation with a therapist somewhere down the road.

Brad's girlfriend, Deb, has also become a big part of my life over the past few years. She has given me the gift of knowing what it is like to have a daughter, even if I did miss the feminine growing up years. Maybe that's a good thing...

My much older brother and sister, Jim & Lois, may live three thousand miles away, but we share the common bond of growing up in the family that put the f-u-n in dysfunctional. No one else could ever understand me the way they do.

My long-time friends, Peder, Roy, Lars, and Wayne give me the gift of their presence in my life. They always seem to know when it's time to make me stop and smell the coffee (or the beer). It doesn't matter how far apart we may be, or how long it's been since we last saw each other, it always seems like we are always together.

I am in a very unique business that puts me together with so many others trying to entertain the world with our words. Many of them have become good friends. As always, Lynn Johnston of *For Better Or For Worse* fame, and best-selling authors Ridley Pearson and Dave Barry, inspire me with their skill. I cannot thank them enough for their friendship and encouragement.

Nancy Warren and I may write in very different genres, but I could not ask for a better friend in this business. I'm in awe of someone who could write a romance based on NASCAR. I'd tell you the story about the two of us and the swans, but she says if I did she'd have to kill me.

Singer-songwriter Greg Greenway has become a very good friend and colleague. We met on his home turf in Cape Cod in 2005 when he introduced me at an appearance for the Cape Cod Writer's Conference, and quickly came to the conclusion that we wanted to work together. That led to our collaboration on eighteen comedic songs about the life of a writer, ranging from being desperate to be published to being stalked by a deranged fan. We performed it together at the Watermark Writer's Conference in September of 2006. I can't wait to do it again.

I also need to thank my publicist, Margo Bates, a very funny writer in her own right, and all of her staff. It must be hard to convince people that I know what I am talking about.

There's also the folks at AuthorHouse who help turn my words into the book you are holding.

And finally, to you, my readers. Between my books and the newspaper column, you all make doing this worthwhile. Without you, I'd be just another story teller with no one to tell my stories to.

Thank you one and all.

Introduction: I May Be Big, But I Didn't Cause That Solar Eclipse

I have often admitted that I am big for my age. I'm tall and I am wide. With my gray hair and beard, along with that whole 'bowl full of jelly' thing I have working for me, small children often mistake me for Santa Claus.

I tell them I am his younger, better looking brother, Irving Claus.

A few years ago, after a total solar eclipse, a friend, or so-called friend, asked if I had stepped in front of the sun. Let's just say, we really don't want to discuss my full moon, and how well it might blot out the sun.

My size has always been a point of conversation. I hit six feet when I was twelve years old, and added another four inches by the time I was sixteen. My older brother stopped at five-foot-nine, slightly taller than my father. My mother claimed to be five-foot two. The only way she ever approached that height was if she stood on top of the dog. It all served to make my height that much more noticeable.

Just what every slightly awkward, pubescent teenager wants: something to make him more noticeable.

In high school I briefly dated a girl who was taller than me. Other kids called her Amazon, but if they were smart, not to her face or within her earshot. That was before I met and fell in love with Diane, who like my mother, might come close to the height she claims to be if she stood on the dog.

And we have a Labrador retriever.

When I stand by Diane, it just makes it that much easier for people to realize that I am big for my age. My sons even stopped growing an inch or two before they reached my height, but they can thank their mother and her vertically deficient genes for that.

I can't shop in normal menswear stores or departments. Even the ones that do stock a few things for people taller than the average munchkin, seem to have some odd ideas about clothes sizes for the bigger set. One store that I visited had pants that matched my waist size and pants that matched my inseam. They didn't stock pants that matched both my waist size and my inseam. I could be short and fat or tall and thin, not big for my age in both dimensions.

I've written before about my thoughts on the person who designed hospital gowns, most of which are shorter than my shirts. I'm thinking about having a made-to-measure hospital gown custom made for me in some Far East clothing sweatshop. Anyone who has ever shared a waiting room with me probably wishes I already did. Seeing me in a hospital gown is probably something that ends up being discussed in a future therapy session.

The thing is, there are a lot of people bigger than I am. In Louisville, Kentucky I once shared an elevator with a woman who single-handedly exceeded the device's weight limit. I felt downright svelte standing beside her. I was in a restaurant in Washington, where I saw a woman who could not squeeze her entire girth onto a booth seat designed for three people. Her food intake helped me suppress my appetite, and proved to everyone in the place that her size had nothing to do with the oft-cited excuse of 'it's a glandular condition.'

Her grease intake could have lubricated a fleet of Mack trucks.

When I visit one of those stores that sell very large clothing, I am happy that I take the smaller sizes. On one visit, I accidentally picked up a pair of men's 8XL bikini-brief underwear, when I was looking for boxer shorts. If you sewed up all the openings and filled it with helium, you would have a giant balloon float for a gay pride parade.

So yes, I may be big, but I didn't cause that solar eclipse.

Friends, Family, Citizens, and Other Forms Of Wildlife

The Future Came. I Expected There'd Be Oatmeal Cookies

Math was never one of my favorite subjects. Perhaps this dislike for numeric problems started when a teacher somewhere back around grade three or four made me calculate just how old I would be in the year 2000. If learning math could depress a nine-year old by making him realize that he'd be forty-seven at the turn of the century, then maybe it wasn't the subject for me.

So here we are... uhm... forty-seven minus nine... uhm... plus seven... uhm... borrow one from the four...

OK, let's just say it's over forty years later.

The year 2000 has passed us by and I don't feel all that different. I'd still like to be able to come home and smell my mother's oatmeal cookies warm from the oven, and go tobogganing on the hill down the street until dinner time. I guess my inner child has survived pretty well. My outer middle-aged white guy hasn't done nearly as well. I look like I just might have eaten a few too many of Mom's oatmeal cookies, and if you put me on a toboggan serious harm might befall anyone else on the hill. Depending on the length of the hill, I just might break the sound barrier, along with a couple of the more important laws of quantum physics.

Looking at that block of time from the other end is only slightly easier than it was to imagine it when I was nine. Then I imagined all of the things I would do in those years. Today I look back and imagine all of the things I could have done but didn't because there would always be time for it "later." Later has come and gone. I still haven't played on a winning Stanley Cup hockey team. (For that matter, my Toronto Maple Leafs haven't won one since 1967, either.) I never learned to fly a plane. Heck, I'm not even close to being the gazillionaire I'd expected to be by now.

Somehow, in my childish forecast of the future, my parents were going to be here with me. The immortality children feel includes the people around them. I expected to see my father ringing in the new millennium, and somehow he'd still be wearing those same baggy shorts he always wore. My mother would still be claiming to be 5'2", a height she could only attain if she stood on the dog.

Dad died in 1982. Scarcely six months later, my mother was gone too. She took her oatmeal cookie recipe with her.

On the other hand I have succeeded at achieving some of the things I imagined back then. I've owned a couple of sports cars over the years. I've been to Disneyland. I've even seen naked women like the ones in the Playboy magazines my older brother didn't do a very good job of hiding in his bedroom.

I don't know what I expected in the way of a wife and children when I was nine. Odds are I wasn't overly attracted to the opposite sex at that age. Perhaps I just hoped for someone who would bake oatmeal cookies while I went tobogganing after work. I guess I lost out on that one. My wife doesn't bake oatmeal cookies. Still, even though I live in an oatmeal cookie-deprived state, I really did luck out when it came to the family I have around me forty-whatever years later.

Between dating and marriage, Diane and I have now seen over thirty New Year's Eves. She has been at my side for all of those years, and I don't think she really cares if I never won the Stanley Cup, learned to fly, or became anything close to a gazillionaire. Our cups hold coffee not champagne. I feel like I'm flying when I'm with her. The gazillion memories she has given me are worth far more than a gazillion dollars (especially Canadian ones).

I am lucky to have my two sons, even though I didn't picture them being here when I tried to do that math problem back in 1962. They've made the two-thirds of those thirty-whatever years an awful lot of fun.

I accurately predicted one part of my present day life. I knew at nine that, no matter what, there would be a dog in my life. There have been three, a brilliant border collie, the dumbest dog to ever get lost on a single flight of stairs, and now Tara, my Labrador retriever assistance dog. Each has been the epitome of loyalty, sleeping at my feet while I write, offering to help me cut down on my eating by sharing whatever I might be eating, and making sure I have a head to pat whenever I needed it.

Despite missing the mark on some of my childhood predictions, I quite like my life today.

I just expected there to be a lot more oatmeal cookies.

Vegas Is An Alarming Place To Go For Rest And Relaxation

After spending most of the year traveling around Canada and the United States, I really need a vacation. I want a few days to relax and regenerate in peace and quiet. Somehow, in my twisted sense of logic, I thought Las Vegas might be the place to find it, so Diane and I slipped away for a few days of fun and sun in the desert.

We quickly remembered what I am sure most of you already know. Las Vegas wasn't the place to go for a rest. There was just too much to do.

We had no intention of spending a lot of money gambling, but the lights and bells of the casinos had a hypnotic, luring effect. We played on the slot machines in the morning, in the afternoon, and at night. We never got far enough ahead to make the effort worthwhile. Each time one of us was winning, the other was losing. In the end, we broke even, which is probably better than most of the people around us. Still, it would have been nice to be one of those people on the plane home who had an extra couple of thousand dollars in their pockets.

I expected Las Vegas to have a lot of flashing lights along The Strip and in the casinos. I didn't expect to have them in my hotel room. At 1:30 AM on our first night, the fire alarm went off in our room. It combined a strobe light just slightly dimmer than the combined candlepower of every lighthouse in New England, with a horn that made the red alert warning on the Starship Enterprise sound like Yanni playing a lullaby on his pan-flute.

It's amazing what a person can do after waking up to sounds and lights like that. I have to say I was quite impressed with the gymnastic maneuver Diane displayed as she went from sound asleep and prone to barely awake and upright beside the bed. Most judges at the Olympics would have given her a 5.8 or 5.9 for artistic merit and technical skill. Factoring in that she is thirty years older than most Olympic gymnasts and that she didn't wake up until after she was almost to the door made her moves all the more awe-inspiring.

I was not nearly as nimble. After beating the alarm clock to death I realized it was the fire alarm. Several thoughts raced through my mind. We were just down the street from the MGM Grand hotel that had suffered a serious fire a few years ago; we were on the 11th floor, above the range of the fire department's ladders, and therefore, we were all going to die.

Diane and I quickly threw on some clothes. If the fire department was going to find my body in the rubble the next day, I wanted to be in more than my underwear. A crowd of people, and a foul stench that didn't resemble any smoke I'd ever encountered met us in the hall. The hotel staff reported the smell came from the water that had sat for years in the sprinkler system's pipes, and there was no fire.

Apparently a bride had hung her wedding dress from the sprinkler nozzle, snapping it off and causing the whole commotion.

I have to wonder if the honeymooning couple even noticed the sirens or the flashing lights. If they did, did they just think it was a natural side effect of their wedding night bliss? If that's what they are expecting every time they climb into bed for the rest of their married life, they're in for a big disappointment.

Perhaps it was all a hoax on the part of the hotel management. Maybe that night was just our floor's turn to be awakened in the middle of the night, so we would go downstairs to the restaurants and the casinos to spend and gamble away a pile of money. With 30 floors of rooms there could be an alarm on each floor once a month. If that was their plan, it worked. Diane and I spent the next two hours spending in the restaurants and gambling away a pile of money in the casinos.

Isn't that just what you would have expected from me? Other people can go into the casinos and win thousands of dollars. Other people can buy the right lottery ticket numbers. Other people can pick the horses that pay huge returns on a $2.00 bet. Diane and I never have any luck.

...unless, of course, you count over spending thirty years of making each other laugh and not being burned to death in our hotel room lucky.

Every Generation Has Its Own Good Old Days

Times were tough back in the good old days. When I was a boy we didn't have the luxuries kids today seem to take for granted.

Oh Good Lord! I'm starting to sound like my father!

I was regularly victimized by my father's memory of how much worse things were when he was a kid. To be honest, I'm not really sure if my father ever was a kid. I think he was born forty years old. Like most parents, he often regaled us with stories about how snowstorms were so much worse when he had to walk uphill both ways to school. Apparently the snow he was forced to trudge through was usually up over his hips. I always chalked that up to the fact that my father wasn't a particularly tall man. Winters were colder. Summers were hotter. They didn't have TV. Food was scarce. Toys were scarcer. Yadda, yadda, yadda, yadda...

Of course he occasionally would revel in the glory of his good old days. Food was cheaper. Music you could understand, not like this "yeah...yeah...yeah" stuff. Mind you, I've never had a reliable explanation for what was being said in that "mareseatoatsanddoe seatoatsandlittlelambseativy" song he sang.

I suppose I should be more like my father. I should educate my sons about just how tough things were in comparison to the way they have it now. I should also lecture them about all of the ways my late teens were better than theirs.

Everywhere you look these days there are things that are virtual. Virtual shopping. Virtual fish in virtual aquariums. There is even, if you are so inclined, virtual sex, and that doesn't even include the people taking Viagra. Kids today have virtual reality. I was their age in the late sixties and early seventies.

We barely had real reality in those days.

If we found we were getting too close to reality, we had certain types vegetation to ingest that could keep it largely at bay. Is it any wonder we couldn't understand "mareseatoatsanddoeseato atsandlittlelambseativy," but we had no difficulty capturing the essence of what Bob Dylan was saying? Future presidents were warned not to inhale though.

The only thing we ever had that was virtual was television reception. If you were lucky you could virtually get four or five stations to appear on your TV in various shades of gray and white snow. I was eight years old before I realized the people in Buffalo, NY saw colors just like we did in Toronto. I assumed everything there was monochromatic because that's what I saw on the Buffalo TV stations. Often virtual reception was dependant on someone going out to the chimney to jiggle the antenna wires.

Just look at the job opportunities available for kids today. I started my career in the newspaper business in the circulation department of a biweekly paper.

In other words, I had a paper route.

Today, teenagers are becoming multi-millionaires by manipulating the Internet for fun and profit. They don't have to spend hours pulling a wagon in freezing rain. The worst thing that might happen to them is getting bought out by Microsoft or Google for $1-billion and stock options.

Life was a lot less confusing back then. When we were kids, men were from Earth and so were women. Somehow in the ensuing 30 years women started coming from Venus and men had to emigrate here from Mars. It all sounds a bit too much like a cheap horror movie to me.

I could have sworn I was still on Earth when my sons arrived. I didn't see a spacecraft deliver them to the hospital, although that could be because I had stopped ingesting those certain types of vegetation in 1972. Come to think of it though, my wife did behave a bit like an alien creature during the delivery, but that's another story.

Back then we didn't worry about what we ate. No one tried to tell us to eat more fiber. We ate meat and potatoes, and drowned the whole plate in gravy, and we didn't feel the least bit guilty about it. Now I feel guilty just looking at the gravy boat in the cupboard. I don't eat butter. I forget what fried foods taste like, and I've been tricked into eating tofu a couple of times.

I never really believed my father about the waist deep snow. I don't think my sons believe me about life before the arrival of color TV, microwave ovens and the home computer. Down the road, their kids will probably doubt life could even exist with the hardships they are enduring here at the beginning of the twenty-first century where some people still eat broccoli.

I'm Not Wrong, Just Psychically Mistaken

I heard it again last weekend. Every once in a while husbands are faced with a dilemma – one that gives them little hope of making the right move. It all stems from a simple little phrase, not even a complete sentence, uttered by our spouses, in response to a simple little question that we pose.

Husband: "Where would you like to stop for lunch?"

Wife: "I don't care - wherever you want to go..."

Eight out of ten husbands know right away they are in trouble the instant their wives respond with those words. The other two are probably newlyweds who haven't had enough marital miscommunication experiences to quite figure out the correlation between ignoring the true meaning of the response and being in trouble.

At best, "I don't care - wherever you want to go..." really means something along the lines of "Let's see if you can psychically determine where it is you had better want to go." At worst it means, "If you really love me, you'll know where I want to go."

Ninety-seven percent of all husbands will not be psychically in tune with their wives' nutritional desires and will make the wrong choice. The other three percent aren't psychically in tune with their wives' nutritional desires either. They are just lucky enough to guess right.

I suppose, after being married for over thirty years, I should be better at determining just exactly where "wherever you want to go' might be, but I'm not. If I assume that I would like to go somewhere that I could place my order without leaving the car, speaking to someone who will ask me if I want a hot apple pie with that, I could be terribly, terribly wrong. It could turn out I really wanted to go someplace where my wife could order pasta. If on the other hand, I think I want to go someplace where I can order a drink with my meal, I could discover that I should have known my wife's idea of wherever I might want to go, just involves a burger, a soda, and a hot apple pie.

There are a number of variations on this same theme. For example, I will not go to the video store by myself anymore. If we decide to rent a video, I want to make sure Diane is with me so I know for sure whatever it is I want to see. I like comedy. She likes science fiction. If I go by myself and pick up whatever I think it is I want, it might be something she already saw at the theater when I was out of town, stars an actor she doesn't like, or isn't science fiction. Not being much of a fan of science fiction, I'm constantly amazed at just how often whatever it is I want to see just happens to be about aliens, starships, or time-traveling robots. If I slip up and rent something like a comedy, I can usually be guaranteed of hearing another phrase within moments of the credits rolling.

"I'm glad we didn't pay to see that at the theater."

That's wife-speak for, "You should have known better than to rent that dog of a picture because it didn't have a space ship on the jacket."

The same holds true for TV. If I'm asked, "Is there anything good on TV tonight?" I have learned the proper response is not, "Yes, Dear, there's a hockey game I feel like watching." No matter how much I think I might want to watch that hockey game, I must realize there is bound to be something better on that includes spaceships and aliens. I once tried to say I wanted to watch a program about an alien invasion, but she didn't buy the idea that the aliens were Swedish, Russian, and Czech right-wingers.

I don't want to give the impression I never get my own way, or I'm always in trouble if I pick the wrong thing. Sometimes, if I throw caution to the wind and go with my gut instinct when I hear "I don't care – wherever you want to go..." it all works out fine. Those are also the days I should probably go out and buy a lottery ticket.

As a man and a husband I have long ago learned to accept the fact that most of the time -- and about most subjects -- I will be wrong, mistaken, incorrect, and most likely misguided. I have to wonder though, if I really accept I am wrong, could I be mistaken about that. In that case I'd be right most of the time.

Yeah, right...

Face It. Husbands Are Irresponsibly Responsible For All Domestic Disasters

Disaster can raise its ugly head and strike out at the unsuspecting passer-by with little or no regard to the suffering it might cause.

Every news medium carries stories on a daily basis about disasters that have befallen people around the world. For some, it might be an earthquake, for others a fire. Different parts of the world face different types of disasters. I don't recall ever reading a report of a bull elephant stampede in Topeka. On the same note, I can't remember ever hearing that a tornado has wiped out a trailer park in Mombasa.

Around my house the disasters just don't seem to have any rhyme or reason. Of course they don't. We're talking about my home here. My life doesn't have rhyme or reason. Why then should I expect that my share of disasters might?

Yesterday was no different than any number of disaster prone days I have faced in the past. It all started out innocently enough. Perhaps that's not quite the right word. Any wife reading this will pick up on that inaccuracy. There is no innocence in a disaster that involves one or more men, even if they are only bystanders to the event.

There is only guilt, and plenty of it to share between all the people who can pee standing up.

If a man is present when the cat tracks dirt across the kitchen floor he will get the blame for it, even if the dirt is so small it cannot be seen without an electron microscope. Wives just instinctively know it's there. I'd like to say that I refuse to take the blame because the cat was never trained to go out to the garden, turn on the hose, and wash its feet before coming into the kitchen. I'd like to say I refuse, but I'm smarter than that. I've learned it's best to accept the fact that I was the one who drove our son to the SPCA to pick out that cat, and I didn't ascertain that the cat had the necessary thumb and forefinger dexterity needed to turn on a yard faucet.

Yesterday's disaster du jour involved soapsuds. OK, it involved lots of soapsuds. I wasn't at home when it happened. Anyone unfamiliar with the laws of male responsibility might let me escape on that technicality.

But no.

It was my fault. It was almost totally my fault. The only thing that saved my butt from accepting the complete responsibility was that my son, another male, was involved. Sons however, have a special relationship with their mothers. A boy can make his mother as mad as a wet she-bear on steroids, and will still only take a small portion of the blame. That's what the boy's father is there for.

In this case Brad put regular dishwashing liquid into the dishwasher instead of the clearly labeled dishwasher detergent. If you've never seen what dishwashing liquid does in a dishwasher you really have missed one of the most spectacular displays of exponential growth known to man. A capful of dishwashing liquid in the sink can make a pretty healthy pillow of soapsuds. Filling the detergent dispenser in a dishwasher with that same liquid creates the monster from the soapy lagoon right there in your kitchen.

Like I said, I wasn't home at the time this disaster was set into motion. How then could it be largely my fault? Oh, dear readers, let me count the ways:

1) Naturally I should have remembered to turn on the dishwasher myself the previous night;
2) If not then, before I went out the next day;
3) When I remembered the dishes needed to be washed before we could eat dinner, I should have turned around, come home, and turned on the dishwasher;
4) If I was dumb enough to telephone our son to ask him to turn on the dishwasher I should have ascertained that he was awake enough at two o'clock in the afternoon to comprehend the difference between dishwashing liquid and dishwasher detergent; and,
5) I never should have tried to say it wasn't my fault.

If I'd been really smart, I would have found a way to get rid of the soapsuds, leaving the kitchen floor sparkling clean. That way, when my wife came home, I could try to get credit for washing the kitchen floor all on my own.

I could have said, "Look, dear wife. I, your ever diligent husband, have washed the floor because there was probably an infinitesimal speck of dirt over there by the dishwasher that the cat dragged in."

No. What was I thinking? She wouldn't buy a load of crap like that in a million years.

Never Try To Reason With An Oak

Well, I'm glad some things just don't change with time.

When I was in university I was given some pretty offbeat assignments, all in the name of expanding my horizons, making me think about the bigger picture, and because the professors just wanted to see if we would do some of the things they came up with. I have always been convinced that several of those assignments were concocted during a drug-induced haze.

I could almost hear a couple of my professors saying things like, "OK, OK, OK. Get this, we could ask them to... Are those donuts for everybody? OK, OK, OK, then they could... Have you ever tried chip dip on an éclair? OK, OK, OK, and if they don't do it, we'll give them something harder next time..."

The professors would arrive at class the next day, forgetting the brilliant plan they had conceived between joints, donuts, joints, chip dip, and, did I mention joints? Along the way to class they'd decide to make us try to teach white mice how to play basketball.

I kid you not. In my second year of university, one of my major projects was to teach two white mice to play basketball. I'm proud to say that George and Ernie were better than all of the draft picks selected by the short-lived Vancouver Grizzlies. If I'd only known then what I know now, I'd have signed them to long-term contracts and acted as their agent.

Another of my projects involved proving the safety of drunk driving. That was for a statistics course, and it served to make me doubt all statistical data that has ever been reported since then. In essence the theory was that since, at the time, roughly forty percent of all traffic related injuries and fatalities involved drunk driving, therefore approximately sixty percent of all injuries and fatalities were the result of drivers who were sober. The conclusion drawn from those statistics was that it was indeed approximately twenty percent safer to get behind the wheel of your car after consuming copious amounts of alcoholic beverages.

Of course, everybody knows 78.6325% of all statistics are made up on the spot.

My youngest son asked if he could borrow my car a couple of weeks ago. "I have to go and do some research for a term paper."

I was somewhat skeptical that the real reason for his need to use the car had anything to do with research for a university term paper because it was after ten o'clock at night.

"I need to do it now so no one will see me doing it," he said.

"Doing what..." I asked, almost afraid of what the answer might be, and how it might affect my car.

"I have to go and talk to a tree," he said. Then I have to write a term paper about the experience.

Like I said at the beginning, some things just don't change. During my time at university I spoke with quite a number of trees. Some of the conversations resulted because I had walked into a tree on my way home from pub night. Most of those involved some fairly blue language, and even with all the emphasis I could put on my statements I still found it hard to get a straight answer from a birch about why it hadn't moved out of the way when it saw me coming.

I can also remember having several conversations with trees along the side of the road I used to hitchhike to and from the campus. Usually those conversations were about how f-f-f-f-f-freaking cold it was, or about the inconsiderate jerks who kept driving past me in their nice warm cars. The roadside trees never said much back to me but I could just tell by the way they were bowing in the wind that they were laughing at me.

The deciduous are particularly cruel bunch.

In a way I envy Brad. University was, and obviously still is, that time in life when you can do the unusual, question the normal, and tilt at a windmill or two every so often. I still do the unusual, question the normal, and tilt at windmills, but at fifty-three, we are supposed to have gotten past that stage in life.

You get strange looks and people tend to question your sanity when you do those things at my age. Lots of people I know think I am a very strange man for the way I look at life. My wife would be at the top of that list. So, should I be worried?

I think I'll go ask one of the cedars on the front lawn what it thinks.

He's Educated To A Degree

Time flies.

I was thinking about my son's graduation ceremony the other day. He and his classmates gathered in front of family for a solemn procession, wearing the traditional caps worn by graduates for decades.

Well, almost. The caps they wore were made from brightly colored construction paper, perched precariously on their heads, as they made their way to the stage to receive their kindergarten diplomas.

That was eighteen years ago.

Last week, we gathered once again. This time hundreds of people assembled to watch another group of graduates that included my son. Wearing the official cap and gown of his university, he completed another phase of his education.

Brad graduated with honors in English. His thesis was about the Shakespearean characters who interact with the audiences during the plays. It's a topic that has brought him to the point where he is ready to take on life in the sixteenth century.

There are those who don't think much of an arts degree in English. It's been said one of the important lessons English majors must learn is to say, "Do you want fries with that?" I suppose, if you stop there, it may be true. Brad will return to school in the fall in the Faculty of Education to become a teacher.

As I watched the proceedings, I thought back on a number of the educational highlights that had brought Brad to this point in his life. A couple I wrote about at the time bear repeating.

This son showed us early on that he had the ability to write stories that would be memorable to all read them. When he was in the sixth grade, he wrote a story about aliens attacking the Earth. I doubt his teacher will ever forget hat story.

I know I won't.

Brad wrote the story on the computer in my office. He availed himself of the feature that checked the spelling, before printing it and turning it in to his teacher. I learned then it would probably be a good idea to proofread anything he wrote on the computer.

Diane and I were called in to the school by a very distressed teacher, who was offended by the language he had used in that particular story. She had a copy for each of us to read with the offending words circled in bright pink highlighting ink.

She didn't appreciate it, when I read his story and proudly proclaimed, "That's my boy!"

He wanted to say the aliens were attacking earthlings with their eight-foot long tentacles. Unfortunately, he allowed the computer program to correct his spelling in such a way that they were using another anatomical feature to beat the defenseless residents of our home planet into submission.

To this day I can't get the image of those aliens and their eight-foot testicles out of my mind.

I'll bet that teacher can't either.

Brad was also the one who was willing to try new experiences in the quest for education. He once tricked me into thinking I was taking him to an introductory driving lesson shortly after his sixteenth birthday. Instead of steering a Chevrolet, he had made the arrangements to steer a Cessna in an introductory flying lesson. I was none the wiser until we arrived at the flight school.

I was just afraid I would have to accompany him.

There were times when I wondered if we would ever get him to this point in life. I think I am due a lot more credit for the achievement than I am getting. I played a number of important roles in his education. I was his alarm clock, when the electric one beside his bed was not loud enough to wake him in the mornings. When waking took too long, I was the chauffeur who drove him the entire three blocks from our house to the school.

As I watched Brad receive his degree, I was understandably proud, and not just because he was the only graduate to jump and click his heels in the air after shaking hands with the chancellor of the university.

That's my boy.

Goodness Gracious Great Balls Of Frozen Dust Particles

My wife doesn't like dust. Perhaps I should say she doesn't like the dust she can see. If she can't see it, it must not really be there. Dust on top of the refrigerator doesn't exist in her short-person world. I, on the other hand, don't pay much attention to dust, no matter where it is.

The other day when she wrote, "WIPE ME!" in the dust on the TV screen, I got the idea she had reached her breaking point. I was wrong. She reached her breaking point when I said I thought it was OK for her to write or draw in the dust, just as long as she didn't include the date. Thank goodness for my reflexes. I was able to fend off the box of dusting cloths she threw at me from the kitchen with the speed and accuracy of a cruise missile.

Her aversion to dust particles isn't universal. In fact, she'll go to great lengths just to find the best place to look at certain kinds of dust, even at two o'clock in the morning. Therefore, I too got to go to great lengths to look at dust at two o'clock in the morning a few nights ago.

Diane has a keen interest in astronomy. I do not. The dust Diane wanted to look at was floating around in space and colliding with the earth's atmosphere in the form of meteors and fireballs; something called the Leonid Meteor Shower.

Normally nature takes care of me during events like that. Living on the west coast, also known as "the wet coast," we have missed several celestial events due to cloud cover. I wasn't so lucky this time. On the night of the meteor shower, the clouds all fled from the sky.

We set out at midnight to find the perfect spot away from lights that would reduce the number of visible meteors. We ended up at the end of a lonely mountain road, with the car windows and sunroof wide open, watching meteors streak across the sky for a couple of hours.

Did I mention the temperature was hovering around the freezing point? The dog was in her place in the back seat of the car looking at us like we had lost our minds. How do you explain the lure of astronomical events to a Labrador retriever when I couldn't even explain them to myself? Sitting in the cold, with my neck bent back so I could watch the meteors through the sunroof gave me a rather severe pain in the astronomy. At least the cold fresh air kept me awake.

On the way home Diane asked if I had enjoyed it. That's one of THOSE questions, isn't it? It falls into the same category as, "Does this dress make me look fat?" and "If I die will you want to get married again?" There are honest answers, and there are wrong answers, and there are the answers that husbands had just bloody well remember to use when responding to questions like that.

I was able to muster up the right answer but between the hour of the night and the dishonesty of the response it came out in a dull monotone, "It was indeed a spectacular and awe-inspiring display of nature in all its splendor..."

I guess I didn't sound too convincing because a couple of miles further down the road she asked if I had ever seen so many meteors at one time. Again I responded with, "It was indeed a spectacular and awe-inspiring display of nature in all its splendor..."

I think I should be commended for being such a good husband. After all I didn't let my comfort take precedence over my wife's desire to see bits of dust burst into flame as they hit the atmosphere. I didn't even question her sanity for wanting to do it at two o'clock in the morning. (I let the dog handle that.) I think it's important for husbands to encourage their wives to relax and enjoy their hobbies. If that meant freezing at the end of a dark mountain road, so be it.

Fair is fair though, right? I think Diane should have encouraged me to watch the Victoria's Secret Lingerie Fashion Show that aired on ABC last week. From the reports I've read, it proved once and for all Victoria doesn't have too many secrets left, and the ones she's trying to keep under cover don't have much space to hide.

Apparently, the show was indeed a spectacular and awe-inspiring display of nature in all its splendor...

I've Been To Hell And Back

I think I know what men's hell looks like.

It has a couple of chairs and five or six doors. Women go in and out the doors and they are attended to by several others, who scurry back and forth bringing them whatever they ask for,

Insipid music, the kind you would hear in an elevator or at a John Tesh concert plays in the background.

The men, and occasionally a woman who must have done something particularly evil, are forced to sit in the chairs. All the while, everyone knows that just behind the doors, the women are disrobing with great abandon.

I had to endure an hour in that hellish environment on the weekend, but I guess I must have been released for good behavior. Oh, right, we're talking about me. It probably wasn't good behavior that got me sprung, but somehow I managed to get a reprieve.

For those of you who may not have experienced it, male pattern hellness is the husband's seating area near the changing rooms of a women's clothing store.

When men shop for clothes, they walk into a store, try on a suit, pick out a couple of dress shirts to go with it, and for those whose jobs require masochistic torture, a tie or two. The whole process can be finished in a matter of a half hour or so.

My wife likes to use me as a sounding board for her decision-making process when she goes shopping for clothes. As a result, I have a fair amount of experience sitting in those chairs in women's wear stores. Her company Christmas party is coming up and she wanted to get a new outfit for the event, so that's how I came to be sitting in hell on the weekend.

Oh, joy.

She went into the changing room with enough items to clothe a small village. The first outfit she modeled for me was a black skirt, a black top and a black lacey shawl to accessorize it.

I've learned to pick and chose my words carefully when expressing my feelings about a clothing decision she is trying to make. For example, I will not answer the 'does this make me look fat' question.

A friend of mine once made that mistake and replied, "No. It's your great big butt and stomach that makes you look fat."

He's now an ex-husband.

When I saw Diane in the black outfit, my first reaction was to say, "Well, dear, if you're going for the Italian widowed grandmother look..."

That, of course, would have been a very foolish thing to say.

Naturally, I said, "Well, dear, if you're going for the Italian widowed grandmother look..."

In my defense, I've never said there is a direct link between knowing something would be foolish to say and preventing my mouth from saying it.

The temperature in hell seemed to drop perceptibly. There was a lot of muttering coming from their cubicles that involved things like, "she should have left him at home," or "good thing he's not my husband."

When I saw the women who made the 'good thing he's not my husband' comment, I had to agree wholeheartedly. One look at her, and I thought it was a good thing I'm not her husband, too. Diane might use me as a sounding board, but she looks like she might use me as a punching bag.

Diane finally picked a very nice outfit with little or no help from me or my comments. In reality, she has a very good sense for what to wear, so I am never very sure as to why she wants me there to comment. Perhaps, she just wants to see how far I can put my foot into my mouth before I choke on it.

There is also a chance she is attempting to give me some idea of just what hell is going to look like so I will start behaving myself better. It might work, too.

I can't imagine spending eternity worrying about the consequences of saying things like, "Well, dear, if you're going for the Italian widowed grandmother look..."

Of Mice And Men... And Mothers

If you search the internet bookstores for my books, you will find that another Gordon Kirkland has written a number of books. He writes about rodents. I assure you, that's not me. I write about incidents. He writes about rodents. While I am not one of those people who would jump up on a chair if a mouse scampered across the floor, I try to avoid contact with them.

My mother had a mind numbing fear of anything on four legs that was smaller than a cat. One particular instance of her getting a little too close to a hamster stands out in my mind.

When I was in high school, we lived in an apartment building with hot water pipes running along the exterior walls for heat. Our unit had a small kitchen with one doorway leading into the dining room and another into the hall by the front door. We had a portable dishwasher that blocked the latter doorway when it was not in use.

Our neighbor, a teacher at my school and a man of somewhat eccentric characteristics had a party one night. Someone brought along a couple of hamsters and a cat and threw them onto his floor to see what would happen. One of the hamsters survived the ordeal by running onto the heating pipes. It spent the next several days moving from apartment to apartment.

A day or two later, my mother looked up from her meal and saw two small beady eyes staring out at her from inside the heating register. As I recall, when she screamed I filled my sinuses with milk, but that's another story. I turned to see what she had seen. When I turned back to look at my mother, she had vanished.

The dishwasher still sat in its place blocking the doorway, but somehow, my mother, a woman who erroneously claimed to be five-foot-two, had cleared it in what must have been an Olympic style vault. To this day, I am sorry I looked the other way and missed seeing that maneuver.

My father did not share her fear of small furry animals; he just preferred they stayed in the forest where they belonged.

Dad wore baggy white shorts that had been part of his Navy uniform, when he puttered around our summer cottage. One weekend, as he snoozed on a lounge chair outside, a chipmunk decided to explore the inner sanctum of those shorts.

My sister and I watched in awe as my father performed an early rendition of Riverdance after waking up with a chipmunk in his boxers.

One of the first apartments Diane and I lived in was also home to several mice. The landlord's solution was to deliver a can of insect repellant. I'm not sure if his comprehension of the English language was sufficient to understand the mice did not have wings.

I did try the insect repellent on the biggest spider I have ever seen, when we discovered it making itself comfortable under the covers of our bed. I think the spider just laughed.

Diane, the world's greatest sufferer of arachnophobia, cried.

We moved the next week.

When my oldest son was ten or eleven he managed to cajole, beg, and plead long enough that his mother and I eventually gave in and bought him a hamster. The smell in his room was horrific, but I think the hamster eventually got used to it.

It was not replaced when it went to live with Jesus after an all night marathon on its exercise wheel.

Despite my past experiences with rodents, I would never think to set one on fire, but, according to the Associated Press story that crossed my desk this morning, 81-year-old Luciano Mares of Fort Sumner, New Mexico, decided that was the best way to get rid of a mouse that he caught in his house.

This was not Lucky Luciano.

He threw the mouse into a pile of burning leaves. The mouse caught fire and ran back to the house, igniting it. No one, other than the mouse, was injured in the blaze, but the house and all of the contents were totally destroyed.

At least it didn't run up his pant leg.

I Am A Romantic Legend In My Own Mind

Spring is the time we are all supposed to start thinking about love and all that other romantic stuff. I, of course, am extremely romantic all year round.

At least I think I am.

Others, including the person who has been on the receiving end of my romantic overtures for the past thirty-some years, tend to raise their eyebrows at that thought. For some reason, I am not what comes to mind when they think of a hunk of burning love.

They do say I'm a big hunk of something, though.

Diane and I met in the late Sixties, but it wasn't until 1971 that we actually started dating. Our first date was September eleventh of that year. Now Al Qaeda has gone and stolen that date from us. It's hard to say you are going to celebrate anything on September eleventh.

It was an incredibly romantic event. I arranged to meet her in a hot spot. You have to remember we were both in high school, so the only hot spot that fit the budget was the laundry room of the apartments our families lived in at the time.

After that, we were virtually inseparable. When people saw one of us, they also saw the other. People laughed at the twelve-inch difference in our heights as we walked along together. It was the only way they could tell we weren't joined at the hips.

My hips were roughly parallel with her biceps.

That difference is just as pronounced today. I may still be big for my age, but Diane is still short for hers.

I was thinking about those early days recently. My youngest son, Brad has been dating the same girl for several years. He and Deb, like Diane and I before them, would be joined at the hip if it weren't for the height difference.

And that's a good thing. Deb has become a big part of our family.

When Brad was about to enter this world, a nurse asked me if he was our first. I said, "No. He's our last." As a result, Diane and I never had the opportunity to have a daughter. Two children were enough. I can't imagine the effect on our financial instability if we'd had to feed more than that.

Still, we missed a lot by not having a daughter. I watched friends and family go through the joys and stresses of raising girls, and came to realize it was a very different experience to what we were going through with two boys. It wasn't better or worse, just different.

The four of us were heading across the border into Washington State a few days ago. The Customs officer at the border looked at our identification and then asked if there was a relationship between the three Kirklands in the car and the one MacKenzie. Brad summed it up in just one word.

"Yes!" he said emphatically.

The officer understood the relationship immediately. No further explanation was necessary. He was happy with Brad's response. Deb was especially happy with Brad's response.

Obviously, he gets that romantic stuff from me.

They are about to head out on a post-university graduation adventure; leaving in a couple of weeks for a six-week tour through Europe to celebrate surviving their undergraduate studies. They've saved diligently for the trip. Deb's father is giving them the airline tickets for graduation gifts and we are giving them Eurorail passes. They'll stay in hostels in France, Italy, Greece, England, Ireland and several other points in between.

Diane and I will be taking the trip vicariously. It's always something we wished we had done, but life got in the way and we kept postponing it. We've now postponed it for nearly thirty-three years. Historic sites Brad and Deb will be seeing on their travels were new when Diane and I might have made the trip.

Being the romantic I am, I'll remind Diane that we might not have had six-weeks in Europe, but it doesn't beat evening in a hot laundry room.

And if that doesn't prove I'm a big old hunk of burning love, I just don't know what will.

With A Friend Like That

One of the things people often worry about when they are around me is that anything they do or say might end up in a column, or in one of the stories in a future book.

I don't know why they wonder. In fact, anything they do or say, just might end up being written about. No wondering is necessary.

That comment came up at lunch today. I am back in the city where I spent my high school years. I still have a lot of friends living here, and try to see some of them whenever I get back. Peder - who doesn't spell his name that way to distinguish himself from all the Peters in the world, but because, through no fault of his own, he's Danish - was my best man when Diane and I were married in 1973.

His sister-in-law apparently warned him to be careful, because I might write about something he said over lunch. Just to show her, I've written about what she said.

I suppose I can understand people being concerned about potentially giving me column material. My family has always been more than a little nervous about that. I still don't know what happened during my son's driver's exam ten years ago, because he swore his mother to secrecy, for fear I would write about it.

All I know is he needed to retake the driver's test a few weeks later.

There is a lot I could write about Peder. When you've known someone for over thirty-six years, there are bound to be a few stories floating around.

I met him when I started grade eleven. We were in the same physics lab. I was in the back of the class trying without a great deal of success to understand the various theories and theorems. He was at the front of the class. He understood physics, which was probably a good thing, because he was at the front of the class for a very important reason.

He was the teacher.

It might seem odd in today's world of Mary Kay Laterno and other less than appropriate student-teacher relationships, for a student and a teacher to be good friends, but 1969 was a different time and we were both spending our days in a very different school.

Good old Oakridge Secondary was populated by a young teaching staff, interested in many of the same things as their students, ranging from sports to music.

I was lucky to be a student there at that time.

I used to hitch-hike to school because there were no busses and the school was a couple of miles from my home. More often than not, Peder pulled over and picked me up. That was good for a number of reasons. It made sure I got to school on time, and didn't have to explain my tardiness to the vice-principal. Of far greater importance was the fact Peder drove an MG, and it was much better to ride in a cool car than some salesman's old sedan.

I can't imagine a teacher picking up a student today. There are just too many liability issues, and I'm sure most school boards have rules against it. It's too bad. Those rides helped foster a friendship that has lasted longer than any other I have ever had.

I've often said that I am a writer today because of the encouragement of my senior year English teacher. Peder gave me some quite different encouragement. One thing was to forget any thought of a career that involved understanding physics. More importantly, Diane and I got married when we were still in university because Peder pointed out we were silly to wait until after school, when we were going to get married anyway.

He even found the priest to perform the ceremony for us.

As I said, I was lucky to go to that school. I'm lucky to have had a friend like Peder for so many years, even if my word processing program tries to tell me I am making a spelling mistake every time I type his name.

The lottery, I'm not so lucky with...

Everyone Needs A Good Movement From Time To Time

I'm Going To Have A Movement

After six years of waking up every morning and wishing it would happen, I am finally going to have a movement.

I'm sure you can imagine what it is like to have lived for so long waiting for something like that to happen. The emotional distress alone has been incredible.

Six years ago, when I had my last movement, it resulted in a considerable reduction in my personal space. It was quite spectacular, in a disturbing sort of way. I'm hoping this next movement will reverse a lot of the effects of that last one,.

The worst part is every time I have a movement it gets more expensive. This one is probably going to cost close to half a million. My first, back in 1975 was less than forty thousand.

Clearly, inflation has had a significant impact on my movements.

Of course, I am not talking about the kind of movements that cause nurses come into your hospital room and ask you if you've had one today. I mean the kind where you have to change addresses.

We've decided to find a new home.

Six years ago, we thought we had an empty nest. Diane was about to make a major career change, and we had a large house and yard to take care of. We decided it would make sense to move into a condominium apartment. It seemed like a good idea at the time.

The same can be said for the idea to develop an atomic bomb.

I have hated living in an apartment since the second day here. I was too busy unpacking on the first day to think about it, otherwise I probably would have decided I hated it on that day, too.

I am not an apartment person. My favorite house was one we owned in the 1970's that had three acres of land and was surrounded by hundreds of acres of open farmland. Outside our apartment is a deck that is approximately four one-thousandths of an acre, surrounded by other equally spacious decks.

In the apartment, at any time of the day or night, there are other people living immediately beside and above us. Thankfully we're on the ground floor, or there would be people below us, too. I have never felt like there is even the remotest iota of solitude anywhere around here. I hear their music, televisions, and conversations.

For a few years we also heard the upstairs neighbor whenever she was having a really good time. She had a really good time just about every night, and could probably be heard all over town and by all the ships at sea. We started sleeping with industrial strength earplugs, but she could still be heard - just a bit muffled.

Thankfully, she had a movement a couple of years ago.

Making the decision to sell your home sets off an unusual chain of events. The first things you think of doing are a whole series of the changes to the place to make it seem more desirable. In the few days since we made the decision to move, our lives have been consumed with doing just that.

I mustered up all of my limited handyman skills and fixed the crack in the plaster where the wall jumped out and tripped one our alternately occupying sons when he came home from a party at least two, if not three, sheets to the wind.

We've rented a second off-site storage locker to put some of the larger pieces of our furniture away until after the place sells. That way, it will seem much bigger to anyone who comes for a viewing.

We even went out and bought a futon for the son who currently occupies the bedroom that was supposed to be my office. His old bed took up over half the room. That way, it will look like you could actually swing a cat in there, should any potential buyer have a penchant for cat swinging.

I've never tried flinging a cat, but I bet it sounds just like the former upstairs neighbor, when she was having a particularly good time.

We Don't Really Live Here Anymore

Selling your house is a trying affair. There are so many things you forget to think about in the heat of the moment when you finally reach the end of your rope with your current accommodations.

One of the joys of buying and selling a home is that it puts you in touch with those wonderful people who have managed to pass the real estate sales exam. Like many people in this situation, I think they fall into two categories, my agent and scum. (Of course, when I said that in my newspaper column, a number of Realtors wrote letters to the editor saying that I had besmirched their entire profession. I wasn't trying to besmirch their entire profession, just the ones who behaved like scum... and the ones who write letters about me to editors.)

We've had a troop of the latter category going through our place over the past few days; each leaving their business card on the kitchen counter. It would have been nice if one of them had also left a note saying something along the lines of, "I was trying to see if I could use your bathroom towel rod as a ballet pole and I pas-de-deuxed it right out of the wall."

That repair was almost too much my handyman skills, to say nothing of the fear it causes for my wife whenever I pick up a screwdriver.

Another agent brought us an offer so low I wouldn't have accepted it last year. He had several justifications for the low offer. Of course, first and foremost was the one all real estate agents fall back on, "I am duty-bound to deliver any offer my client might choose to make."

They never finish that statement to make it entirely truthful by saying, "...that I told them they should make."

One of the worst parts of selling a home is the fact you have to keep the place looking like no one really lives here. You never know when you are going to get a call from your agent telling you a prospective buyer will be arriving in an hour.

No matter how hard you try, life goes on around here. Dishes get used. Beds get slept in. Showers get taken. It would be OK if it was just Diane and I. We could get the dishes to the dishwasher, the beds made, and the shower stall wiped down. Our son, who seems to be convinced the entire process has been put in motion to inconvenience him, is another story.

One day last week, I missed a call from our agent asking for a showing time. Instead of waiting for confirmation, the other agent just showed up unannounced. I was in the middle of getting a wall ready to be painted to cover the nail holes in the area that used to hold a display of family pictures. (Apparently, when you are selling your home you are not supposed to let anyone know the people selling the house have family.) I was also working on the lyrics to three new songs for my show next month, and since we had dismantled my office to make that room look bigger, my laptop and notes were spread across the living room sofa.

Of course, Mike had taken a shower just three or four hours before, so naturally the bathroom floor was still covered in dirty laundry and wet towels.

Thankfully, there is another unit for sale in the building and the agent offered to take his client there first, giving me an opportunity to set a new land speed record trying to make the place look like no one lives here.

I was reasonably successful. The agent and his client came in, took one pass through the place and left. I didn't even have time to get my shoes on and leave the unit so they could look at it alone. The agent let it slip that he and his friend were having lunch and decided to just have a look at what was on the market. They weren't really an agent and a potential buyer after all.

I had straightened up, shut off my laptop, and plucked my sons underwear from behind the bathroom door for nothing.

You'd be proud of me. I followed one of the other rules at that point. When you are selling your home you aren't supposed to tell a real estate agent which end of the horse you think he best personifies.

But you can think it.

Homing In On The Search Of Home Ideas

My wife and I decided to visit a home and interior decorating show recently. We've bought a new house and are looking for ideas. Some things we want to do with the new place are obvious, others are open for discussion.

For example, as soon as we take possession of the new house, the movers will be told they are to simply put the living room and dining room furniture in the middle of the room, because painters will be arriving the next day to change the color of the walls in those two rooms. Combined the two rooms are twenty-eight feet by fifteen feet, and they are painted in one color.

One hideous color.

On its own it is a fine color. Whenever I have an upset stomach, I open the medicine cabinet and look for that color. Somehow though, I cannot see myself sitting comfortably at the dining room table surrounded by Pepto-Bismol® pink.

I think it might send a subliminal message about the quality of the food I'm eating.

Wandering around the inside of a football stadium filled with booths offering everything from hardwood floors to custom made mahogany dog food bowl holders, shows that, while some companies have made it into the twenty-first century, others are still anchored mid-way through the last one.

A company selling irons had a sign in their display that said, "Your husband called and said you could buy this iron."

I may from time to time be a bit on the chauvinistic side, but I would never have survived thirty-three years of marriage if I had been saying what my wife could or could not buy.

The only way a sign like that would have any relevance in our house would be if it said, "Your wife called and said you should do your own damn ironing."

I wish these shows would limit the number of carnie wannabes. There seemed to be at least one in every aisle, hawking some new product that would purportedly change our lives if we would just liberate $49.95 from deep within our wallets. These people all had microphones attached to their heads and let loose with an endless high-volume dissertation about never-need-sharpening knives, brooms that collect dust, pet hair and cookie crumbs with an electrostatic charge, and miracle dusters that clean blinds, hard to reach corners and the lint from your dryer hose. All conversation had to stop whenever you got within fifty feet of one of their booths, because no one in the vicinity could possibly talk over top of the prattle.

For the most part we are in agreement about what we want to do with the new house. We both liked the wide-plank hardwood floors, the granite countertops, and the wood and stone fireplace walls. We also both agreed that there would be no room in the new house for the life-sized statue of a buffalo.

The eight foot tapestry of the last supper was also near the top of both our, "I don't think so" lists, as was the entire selection of paintings in the 'everything under $50.00' booth. Most of them looked liked they had been painted by drunken monkeys.

That's not to say there are still some differences in the way we look at things. We have decided that the move will be a good time to replace the living room furniture. For Diane that means new sofas and chairs. I'm thinking more in line with a fifty or sixty-inch flat-screen high definition TV.

After all, you can always watch a hockey game while sitting on the floor.

I finally relented and tried out a leather sofa complete with reclining footrests. After walking around the show floor for an hour and a half on my crutches, I thought I might just spend the rest of the day there. I asked the exhibitor if she would mind just crating me up at the end of the show and shipping me back home.

She declined.

We came away with a lot of really good ideas to put into our new home, and one rather sizable problem.

How are we going to pay for it all?

Life (And Death) On The Real Estate Roller-Coaster

I've never been a huge fan of boxing, although I have always been a great admirer of Muhammad Ali, especially during the years since he left the ring.

Despite my lack of interest in boxing, I am thinking of little else these days. The kind of boxing I am talking about doesn't involve right upper cuts or left hooks. After a day of it, I still end up feeling like I've had the living beaten out of me, though.

We're boxing up our possessions for our move.

It has been a long and arduous two-and-a-half months since we listed our condo for sale. No theme park could possibly have given us a roller-coaster ride like the one we've experienced.

We listed our place on August fourteenth. That morning a despondent squirrel committed suicide by climbing into the power transformer station that services our town. Power was knocked out for two or three hours. My wife took her hair dryer and curling iron to her office, which is only a few blocks from home.

Our Realtor came over in the evening, and we signed all of the necessary papers. She left at about 9:45. That's when Diane remembered her hair dryer, which she'd need in the morning, so we drove to her office to get it. We were only gone ten or fifteen minutes.

In that time, several police cars, marked and unmarked, arrived at our building. When we returned, the place looked like a scene from Cops. There was an officer in the lobby when we came upstairs from the parking garage.

He looked like he was going to lose his donuts.

A rotund elderly woman from the fourth floor had last picked up her newspaper twelve days earlier. During that time the temperature had been well above normal. Apparently, her apartment was crawling with the sort of infestation you would normally only see on an episode of C.S.I.

This sort of thing happens. There are companies that specialize in containing the problem and cleaning up afterwards. One would think the money we spend on monthly building fees would have paid for a property management company with the brains to advise our building council to insist the woman's family use one of those companies.

One would think.

The family arrived on the scene the next morning and started dragging things out of the apartment, including the mattress on which the woman had spent her postmortem twelve days. They dragged things along the fourth floor hallway, down the elevator, and out through the lobby. They filled the building's garbage bins to overflowing.

That's when the flies started arriving.

It was not the sort of thing you would want to list as a selling feature of your unit.

A few days later, just when we were starting to get some interest in looking at our condo, we received a notice that the building had to be evacuated for twelve hours, so it could be fumigated with pesticides.

I guess I should have expected something like this. After all, few things that can be described as normal ever happen in my household. Usually though, it's my fault.

At least that's what Diane tells me.

Our Realtor was upbeat about it. She told us it was all uphill from there. We had experienced the bottom and would soon be enjoying the heights of a successful real estate transaction.

That's the thing about roller-coaster rides. Just when you think you're reaching the high point, the bottom falls out beneath your feet and you careen back down again. They also leave your stomachs feeling much like that police officer we met in the lobby the night we signed the listing papers.

That odd first night of the experience wasn't the low point. I am convinced it was merely an omen of the experiences that were to come.

Those experiences would leave me, the people we were buying our new house from, and several Realtors involved in the transactions with blood pressure that could have sent the space shuttle into orbit.

But they are another story, and you are going to have to wait until next week to read about them.

The Real Estate Roller Coaster Part Deux

Last week I told you about the ominous beginnings of the real estate roller coaster we've been riding for the past several months, when the police found the body of a woman who had been dead for twelve days in our building. An hour earlier we had signed the listing papers with our Realtor.

It can't get much worse than that – or so we thought.

We found a house we liked fairly quickly, and put in an offer that was accepted. Of course, our offer was conditional on the sale of our condo. Within a week, the seller of the new house received an offer without conditions, so we lost out.

Over the next week we drove past a number of other houses on the market, most of which seemed to sell before we could even get to the stage of looking inside them. Finally we found a house we really liked, and once again put in an offer conditional on selling our place.

That same day an article in the newspaper talked about how the real estate market in our area had peaked and was beginning to slow down. Slow down I could have dealt with. Coming to a complete and utter stop, was a bit more stressful. We went for nearly two weeks without our Realtor getting a single call about our place. In the interim, the selling agent on the house we had the offer on held open houses every weekend, looking for another buyer.

We dropped our asking price twice and finally stirred up some interest. We were elated when we heard there was an offer coming in. After a bit of negotiation, we came to an agreement with the potential buyer. We thought our problems were over.

Funny thing about thinking your problems are over – that's about the point when they seem to get bigger.

Real estate deals often fall apart because a buyer is unable to get financing, something comes up in an engineer's inspection of the property, or some other such cause. Those are the risks you might expect, but if anything is true in this world, my experiences do not necessarily follow expectations.

The deal fell apart because of two inches of canine loftiness.

The buyer's dog was two inches taller than the condo bylaws allowed. We tried reasoning with the building council members, by pointing out that the bylaw says the dog is to be less than twenty inches at the shoulder and they were measuring to the nape of the neck.

That didn't work.

We tried pointing out that it was smaller dogs that caused any dog related problems in the building. I cited the example of the little piece of shitsu that can out-bark an entire pack of foxhounds, and the evidence left behind by a small male dog aiming at the newspaper delivery box.

That didn't work either.

As my stress and aggravation level reached a critical mass, I pointed out that the member of the building council, who was being so strict on the dog height bylaw, lets her dog wander around off leash.

That really didn't work.

Lord Acton may have said that power corrupts and absolute power corrupts absolutely, but he could never have predicted the kind of power that can be wielded by a senior citizen on a condo building committee.

Thankfully, we managed to sell the unit again a few very stressful days later. The new buyer does not own a dog, although I am tempted to start a rumor in the building that I am thankful there is nothing in the bylaws about the height of pet howler monkeys or pythons with a taste for shitzu.

The roller-coaster ride we've been on may not be over just yet, but we don't think we'll feel like we're hanging upside-down on a hairpin turn between now and moving day. The biggest problem we are having now is that it looks like we are living beside the Great Wall of China thanks to dozens of boxes piled in every available bit of floor space.

And we haven't seen the cat in a while.

I Can Pack A Lot Of Stuff Into A Movement

All those who are naïve enough to think all of my hassles of buying and selling a home would end on moving day, raise your right hand.

OK, I have to put my hand down now, because it is too hard to type with just my left hand.

In the first year of writing this column, I wrote a piece called *Much Ado About Stuff*. It had to do with the fact that just about everything in my sons' lives at the time could be summed up with their one favorite word.

Stuff.

They had school stuff. When they went out, they were going to do stuff. Perhaps most perturbing was the green stuff I'd find growing on plates under their beds, whenever I would begin to wonder why we no longer had enough place settings for a dinner for two.

They were teenagers at the time. We no longer have anywhere near that amount of stuff to deal with in our lives. It has more to do with the fact that only one of them still lives with us, than a decrease in their penchant for leaving the remnants of grilled cheese sandwiches on the plates under their beds.

When moving day arrived last week, I discovered my wife and I also have a lot of stuff. In fact, it was enough to fill a five-ton truck to capacity. The movers expected to load up in a couple of hours because we were just moving out of a two bedroom apartment.

They weren't prepared for our stuff.

It took six hours to load the truck. Apparently, they've seen people with less stuff in four-bedroom, double garage, split-level houses.

We only moved five blocks. I was really wishing I could have convinced the movers to charge by the mile instead of by the hour. I was picturing money with wings flying up into the sky, the way it used to in cartoons, with every passing hour.

No matter how prepared you think you are for moving day, there are always last minute items to deal with, and stresses that you could not have predicted.

Diane and I sat in the living room on the night before the move and congratulated ourselves for being so prepared. When the movers arrived, we quickly determined our self-praise was premature. While they started hauling all of our stuff out to the truck, we were madly rushing around the apartment doing all of the things that still needed to be done.

Who knew there could be that many cables to detach from the back of the television set, or that unhooking the internet and telephone would mean having to prostrate myself under a desk for twenty five minutes?

Naturally, we should not have expected the weather to cooperate. Moving day was the coldest day of the year thus far. It rained. It hailed. Even the odd snow flake fluttered to the ground, despite the fact that I thought snow was banned in this part of the country.

When I went to take a load of stuff to the car, I spent ten minutes looking for my coat. Finally, I asked Diane if she had seen it.

She had.

She packed it, and it was already somewhere on the moving van.

"You packed my coat?" I asked trying hard to imagine what logical excuse she could have.

As I have said many times before, I know that no matter what, the meager fact that I am the husband in this relationship means Diane will always have a logical reason for doing absolutely anything. Any doubts I might have about the rationale will be wrong, because if a man speaks in the forest of a marital relationship and there is no one there to hear him, he is still wrong.

Wrong, wrong, wrong, wrong, wrong.

"You must have left it in the packing zone," she said.

I thought about pointing out that the entire place was currently 'the packing zone." I thought about it, but I was smart enough not to say it.

So now I am sitting in the new house; the unpacking zone, if you will.

I still haven't seen my coat.

Is It Just Me Or Does This Kind Of Thing Happen to Other People?

My Christmas Shopping Doesn't Involve Camping

Family Christmas celebrations change as time goes on. We've gone from having Christmases with just the two of us, to the joys of Christmas with small children, to the massive wish lists of older kids, and now on to adult children. Each phase has been quite different.

This is now the twenty-seventh Christmas since Mike was born. That first Christmas with him was filled with new experiences. I learned the hard way I should always read the boxes gifts came in, so as not to be surprised at midnight on Christmas Eve when I discovered those three little words that mean so much:

"Some assembly required."

Some assembly, I could handle, even with my limited handyman skills. Spending three hours in the basement trying to fit wheel A onto axle D of a ride-on car, sapped me of my warm thoughts about the joyous season.

Mike had a great time playing with it on Christmas morning. "It," however, was not the car I had spent the night building, and that I'd sacrificed the skin on my knuckles for, when wheel A slipped off axle D.

"It" was the box the car came in.

As the boys got older, I was glad I managed to escape the insanity of Cabbage Patch Doll pandemonium, and the lunacy of the Tickle Me Elmo shortage. I never had to line up for any of the things they wanted, nor did I ever have to fight another shopper for an annoying, giggling, stuffed animal.

Until this year.

My youngest son would like to add a Nintendo Wii to his apartment décor. If any of you have tried to get one of these things this year, you will know just how futile a pursuit that has become. I thought it would just be a case of visiting my local Best Buy and picking one up off the shelf.

Wrong, wrong, wrong, wrong, wrong.

When I stopped by the store recently, I discovered they were out of stock. I asked the salesman when they might be getting more in.

"Probably Friday," he said, but I noticed he was smirking as he said it.

As it happened, I had to be near the store on the Friday in question for an appointment. I would be able to get to the store just before it opened and still make my meeting on time.

There was a large crowd outside the store when I pulled into the parking lot. When I got close to the door I was able to see a sign that said they had indeed received a shipment of Nintendo Wiis, and were handing out tickets for them on a first come first served basis. I made the mistake of asking a bleary-eyed man where to get one of the tickets.

"You'd have had to be here last night at 5:30 with the rest of us," he said.

I looked at the group that stood around the door, clutching their tickets, and doing the dance that said it had been sixteen hours since they had last seen the inside of a restroom.

"I don't camp in the summer in campgrounds with hot and cold running water," I said, "so I don't think I'd be up for doing it in a parking lot with no running water."

Every time I mentioned the words 'running water,' I noticed several of the group started dancing faster.

It gave me an idea.

"At least you were out of the rain and didn't have to stand in those big puddles," I said.

The dancing sped up even more, and there were a few painful moans from members of the group.

"Lucky you won't have to be here tonight," I added. "The radio says were to get two inches of rain overnight. Those gutters will probably overflow with that much water."

One man screamed and ran for the bushes at the back of the store.

I was really hoping he'd drop his ticket, but I guess after so many hours, it was locked in his grip.

Cruel? Well, maybe a little, but had I succeeded, I wouldn't still be looking for a Nintendo Wii.

Whatever it is.

I'm Just A Speed Demon

Once you get past fifty, you start to think that the firsts you expect to experience might start to wane.

I'm not talking about the first time we experience new technologies, we'll all continue to have those firsts until the first time we experience our own funerals. I mean the firsts that everyone else might have had ten, twenty or thirty years ago. I had one of those firsts on the weekend, and I'm not too happy about it.

I got my very first speeding ticket.

I'm now going to experience another first – fighting my first speeding ticket.

I don't deny I was going over the speed limit. I was traveling with the other drivers who were also going over the speed limit. Had I driven at the posted limit, I would have had a trail of irate drivers lined up behind me, and presented a clear danger to everyone on the road.

I pulled over to the right-hand lane to let a driver pass me who had rapidly approached from the rear. I may have even accelerated a bit to get out of his way quickly.

Ten seconds later, I was the one being waved off to the side of the road by a police officer who looked like he hadn't yet been faced with the need to purchase razor blades.

The officer asked me for my papers and failed to respond when I asked him about the blue Mazda that had just passed me. He walked to the back of the car and wrote the ticket.

The one hundred and ninety-six dollar ticket.

When he passed it to me, I asked again why the blue Mazda was not pulled over when it was clearly going considerably faster than I was. He gave me an answer this time; one that leads me to question the current level of intelligence screening that is being done in recruiting officers.

"I didn't check him."

Let's translate that:
- "I like blue cars."
- "They don't teach multitasking at the police academy."
- "I'm just too stupid to see the other driver was going a lot faster than you."

- "My big brother drives a blue Mazda and he'd beat me up if I pulled him over."

He obviously failed to check all of the other drivers who were traveling down that stretch of road at the same time. I was just the easiest to wave over because I was the one in the right hand lane. He was probably afraid to step into the other lane because he might have been run over by the blue Mazda that he didn't bother checking.

A friend of mine got a ticket thrown out by a judge a number of years ago. He also asked the officer why he was the only one in a line of traffic to be pulled over.

"You were the only one who stopped when I waved," the officer said.

Of course, there are lots of people who get pulled over for speeding who deserve to get ticketed because they let their mouths run free without engaging their brains. A story was related to me when I was down south about a driver from a state north of the Mason-Dixon Line, who had been pulled over for speeding in Georgia.

The Georgia state trooper said, "You can't go through Georgia that fast."

The driver reportedly said, "Well, Sherman did."

Apparently, there are still some people, the state trooper for one, who are still a bit touchy about how fast General Sherman stormed through Georgia a hundred and forty years ago.

Not only did the driver in question get a speeding ticket, but by some miracle, his taillight shattered just as the trooper walked past it on his way back to his cruiser to write the ticket.

I'll have to spend the next few days looking at the ticket under an electron microscope to try to read the ultra-fine print instructions for disputing it.

Hopefully, between now and the court date the officer will experience a few firsts of his own.

His first transfer to a post on Baffin Island, would suit me fine.

I Had My Day In Court

I called my first book *Justice Is Blind - And Her Dog Just Peed In My Cornflakes*. I was given proof last week that she is indeed blind, a little deaf, and her dog still has incontinence issues near my breakfast cereal.

Many people, including several members of my extended family, have always known someday, somewhere, I would be on trial for something. OK, so maybe they expected something a little bit more dramatic than traffic court, but it was a trial just the same.

Last September, I got my first speeding ticket in over thirty years of driving. I felt my speed was justified. I had accelerated in order to change lanes, because another driver was approaching my rear bumper at a much greater speed than I was going.

Having your spine broken in a rear-end collision tends to make you a bit more wary about that sort of thing. The cop didn't see it that way, but I still contend his eyes were glazed over because he was using a radar gun under the influence of donuts.

I learned something in the court case. In this jurisdiction, the only defense a traffic court judge will listen to is if you are driving someone to the hospital in a medical emergency. Apparently, getting out of the way of another driver, whose rate of approach behind you was presenting an imminent danger to the cleanliness of your driver's seat upholstery, is not an adequate defense.

I was prepared for the trial. I was tempted to follow the example Arlo Guthrie set in his song Alice's Restaurant. I considered bringing in forty-seven eight by ten color glossy photographs, with circles and arrows and a paragraph on the back of each one telling what it was.

Instead, I settled for an eleven by seventeen color map of the area with letters clearly showing where I was when I saw the other driver, where he was, and where the officer was hiding. My map provided evidence that the officer had no way of seeing what was going on, because he was hiding around a curve and behind a forest that blocked his vision.

I was proud of that map.

The officer was allowed to present his case first. He talked for seven minutes about his experience as a police officer, his training with the laser gun, how he can determine the actual speed of a car within a very small range using nothing but his eyes and his experience, the weather on the day in question, his route to the speed trap, and several other meaningless details.

I'm not sure if it was for effect, but he did it all in a monotone. I thought for a moment that he might have been about to add some miniscule amount of inclination to his words, but he just needed to clear his throat.

Just as I, along with the judge, the other people waiting to have their cases heard, three people out in the hallway, and the parking lot attendant were about to nod off, Tara. my assistance dog, decided she had heard enough.

She yawned.

A fully grown Labrador retriever can make a great deal of noise when she wants to let the world know she is bored to tears with somebody droning on for so long. The yawn started as a slight whimper, and built in tone and volume until it reached a crescendo slightly quieter than a Boeing 767 before trailing off.

It was almost enough to have us both cited for contempt of court.

In the end, the judge didn't pay any attention to my map, even though it was rendered in full color and printed on glossy paper. She said I had not proven it was necessary for me to speed to get out of the other driver's way, and she found me guilty, but sentenced me to a reduced fine.

If there is a next time, I'm bringing the forty seven eight by ten inch color glossy photographs with the circles and arrows and paragraphs on the back of each one.

And Tara can tell Justice's dog to stay away from my cornflakes.

You Crank And I'll Grump

I received one of those pass-it-on emails the other day. There seem to be a lot of them going around. In this case, the instructions were to 'pass it on to five bright women.' I don't think the sender has any doubt about my gender; however he said he had difficulty identifying five bright women. (For the right price I will supply his name and address to the militant wing of women's liberation movement.)

The email contained a detailed review of all of the reasons women have for being cranky. It would appear that the process of creating cranky women starts when the boys at school snap the straps on girl's training bras, and continues on through dating, marriage, pregnancy, childbirth, and all the way to menopause. There was even a mention of the unfair advantage men have when it comes to relieving themselves in the woods.

In reading this diatribe about how badly women have been treated in life, I came to the conclusion that, while I wouldn't want to deal with some of the issues women have, their reasons for crankiness are just different from the reasons men have to become grumpy.

We put up with a lot getting from the cradle to the grave, too.

I can well imagine how annoying it must be for young girls to have their training bras snapped on the school playground, but what about the sort of thing boys have to deal with. If you've ever played a contact sport, you know the pain that results when your athletic supporter shifts just at the point of contact. For many of us, it's a sheer wonder we were ever able to father children.

I am sure dealing with being pregnant can indeed be a trying time in a woman's life. I can even attest to the fact that it is clearly a cause of crankiness. During a pregnancy, it's all about the woman. Her needs. Her cravings. Her hormonal imbalances. Not enough is ever said about the sheer, unadulterated terror men must live with during a pregnancy.

During the first trimester we discover the sweet, loving girl we married has the ability to turn, in a millisecond or maybe two, into a demonic creature with all the sweetness and joy of a lion with a thorn in its paw.

In the early, childless years of a marriage, we learned there are some questions that are better left unanswered. These usually involve something along the lines of "Do I look fat in this dress?" When pregnancy occurs any question has the potential for explosive reactions of nuclear proportions. Asking questions can be even more dangerous than driving through a minefield.

"Did you have a good sleep, Dear?"

"Listen here, Mr. Fell-asleep-when-his-head-hit-the-pillow, I certainly did not have a good sleep. Between bouts of nausea, the baby kicking, and considering all of the various ways of murdering you for sleeping so soundly, I did not have a good night's sleep. And don't you ever forget that this is all your fault. You did this to me."

"Okay. I'll just be here, hiding under the dining room table, until you give birth."

While raising the children fathers tend to forget about the effects of a hormonal imbalance. We're too busy wondering how two teenage boys could power their way through a month's supply of food before we are even finished unloading the groceries from the car.

Unfortunately, the day soon comes when the hormonal imbalances of our spouses once again bring on a reign of terror. Menopause descends like a fog, consuming any smidgeon of normalcy it finds in its path.

I, like men for generations before me, have discovered that this so called 'Time of Life' is definitely not the time of our lives. Hell hath no fury like a woman who has lost the ability to properly gauge room temperature. I know one guy who nearly lost permanent use of his right hand when he tried to adjust temperature in his car. The fact that frostbite was developing in several regions of his body did not give him the right to turn off the air conditioning and turn up the heat, because his menopausal wife was sweltering through another one of her personal heat waves.

I suppose men really are largely responsible for making women cranky. Cranky women tend to make men grumpy. Therefore, men are also responsible for making themselves grumpy.

Boy, just realizing that is something that really makes me grumpy.

I'm Going To Start Hiding During Full Moons

If I ever had any thoughts about believing the full moon had an effect on the mental functioning of certain individuals, they were confirmed this past weekend. While the moon was technically not quite full it did hit full status on the following Monday, so close enough for horseshoes and idiots.

Clearly some people are just plain stupid, no matter what side of the moon the sun is shining on. Others seem show the highest degree of their stupidity when the moon is full.

I was driving along the main thoroughfare in a shopping center parking lot, when a car shot out from the end of an aisle directly in front of my car. Thankfully my brakes are in good working order and I had tires that were designed to give more traction in the rain.

I hit my horn and my brakes with the same intensity. I did that same thing many years ago in a car that had its horn on a metal ring inside the steering wheel. On that occasion I ended up skidding sideways down the street staring at the metal ring in my hand after snapping it right off the steering wheel.

On this more recent occasion, the woman who drove across my path clearly did not like me honking at her. She rolled down her window and shouted at me that there was no stop sign for her so she had the right of way. This surprised me for a number of reasons.

First off, how many shopping center parking lots put stop signs at the end of every aisle as they meet the main thoroughfare? Isn't it just a given for those drivers with half a brain, they should stop before driving across in front of another driver?

Perhaps even more surprising was the fact that the woman also gave me the classic single finger salute that did not mean she thought that I was number one in her book.

It's not that I haven't gotten that salute before a time or two thousand, but I don't often get it from a woman in her eighties who just caused my antilock brakes to internally hemorrhage.

Later on the weekend I was in a busy grocery store. As always, Tara my assistance dog, was at my side. Her service dog coat grants her entry into establishments that normally discriminate against canine clientele. Even before I had Tara around to help me, I often wondered why some places let in screaming children but still bar dogs.

Tara is a big help to me when we are in a store. I try to avoid bending over as much as possible because since the accident and learning to walk again, I have had a tendency to continue bending until my face hits the floor once I start. Tara can pick up products off the lower shelves and pass them to me. She'd rather do that than try to help me get back on my feet.

As we walked through the store, Tara suddenly jumped forward about three feet. Another shopper had rammed her with his grocery cart. When I turned to see who had done it, the man was actually laughing about it.

It was one of those moments I wished Tara's training included obeying a command to remove someone's testicles. By the look on her face, she was wishing her training hadn't included avoiding giving in to an urge to remove someone's testicles.

"She was probably thinking, "Oh, if only I were a pit-bull right now…"

A similar event occurred several years ago. A woman rammed one of my crutches with her grocery cart.

Rather than apologize she said, "I wouldn't have hit that thing if you didn't have it out beside you like that."

I said, "Well, M'am, If I put the crutches between my legs I tend to fall over, and if I don't bring them at all I am sure to fall over. Neither one is particularly high on my to do list"

It's comforting to know that my Labrador Retriever is a whole lot smarter than some people, and apparently not affected by full moons the way they are.

At Least Clothes Hunting Isn't Dangerous

Let's make one thing perfectly clear. I do not like shopping for clothes. Buying clothes is something I do, just to make sure I do not cause general panic in the streets by not wearing them.

I have often said that I am big for my age. As a result, I have to shop in stores with names like The Humongous Haberdashery or Trousers T-Shirts and Tents. It's rarely a pleasant shopping experience.

I also try to refrain as much as possible from wearing suits. Ties are as welcome around my neck as a noose under the chin of a nineteenth century cattle rustler. Thankfully, in this profession, I don't have to wear suits or ties all that often.

You should all be thankful you will never see me in a kilt. On that, I give you my solemn word.

Sticking to very basic casual wear means I do not have to follow the whims of the fashion police. Jeans and a sweatshirt do not go in or out of style. I don't have to worry about what I wear on, before, or after Labor Day. I may never make it onto one of those best dressed lists, but at least I will be comfortable in my reduced chic level.

I needed a new pair of jeans last week; nothing fancy, just a plain, normal, everyday pair of blue jeans. The kind you find in any department store or men's wear outlet, except in my case, those stores run out of denim before they get to my size.

Actually, many of those stores carry jeans in my waist size. They also carry jeans in my leg length. They just don't carry jeans that are in both my waist size and my leg length. Obviously, you can be short and fat, short and skinny, or tall and skinny. You just can't be tall and fat if you want to get a pair of jeans there.

I'm in that latter category, thus the trip to Mr. Humongous.

Department stores and other men's wear retailers sell those plain jeans for thirty or forty dollars. Sometime you can even find them on sale for twenty. Mr. Humongous sells the same jeans for seventy-five dollars.

When you shop in a regular store, you can find sizes like L, XL, and sometimes even XXL. Stores like Mr. Humongous have sizes that start where the others leave off. You would not believe what a pair of XXXXXXL boxer shorts looks like. I've seen smaller economy cars.

Stitch up the openings on a pair of XXXXXXL men's bikini briefs, fill them with helium and you have a giant balloon for a gay pride parade.

There is one thing that is not oversized by any extent of the imagination in these stores. You'd think a store with a clientele that is taller and wider than other stores, might put in a change room that is also taller and wider.

You might think, but you'd be wrong.

I took a pair of jeans into a change room, slightly larger than the average telephone booth to try them on. Just trying to get my shoes off, took more movements than a rhythmic gymnastics performance.

The salesman came to the door a couple of minutes after I went in and asked how the pants fit.

I said, "I don't know yet. I bent over in here and I'm still trying to get the coat hook out of my butt."

Surely, when these places are charging twice the price for the same products, they could afford an extra couple of square feet in their change rooms. Although, I suppose it would take away from the space needed for those XXXXXXL bikini briefs.

So it really should come as no surprise that I do not enjoy shopping for clothes. Having to pay far more than the average person for a pair of jeans, not to mention performing a do-it-yourself prostrate examination with a coat hook in the change room, just does not make for an enjoyable trip to the mall.

Of course, the weekend could have been a lot worse. I could have been the guy grouse hunting with Dick Cheney.

My Internal Alarm Clock Is Stuck On Snooze

I'm probably clearly identifying my age when I say I have a song by Neil Sedaka running through my head this morning. I'm sure there are more than a few of you who can remember the tune to "Breaking Up Is Hard To Do." Naturally the version I am hearing is more fitting to my current situation. The word 'breaking' has been replaced with 'waking.'

"Because waking up is so very hard to do..."

I think it might have something to do with living so far north in January. At this latitude the sun isn't up until almost 8:00 AM, and it goes down again well before 5:00 PM. When the alarm goes off at 6:00 the room is still in darkness. In my early morning mind a dark room must mean it is still the middle of the night.

There's a chance a couple of gallons of coffee might be helpful, but only if I could have the caffeine distilled and injected intravenously. I make my own coffee to get just the right potency. Even with a full pot all to myself, I am still only awake enough to know I had better not be asleep when all that fluid hits my bladder.

The other reason I am make my own coffee was my New Year's resolution to stop paying ridiculous prices for it at the specialty coffee stores around town. I feel a bit guilty about that though. In the three weeks since I quit buying several servers have been laid off due to the severe downturn in consumption it caused.

You'd think a walk in the fresh morning air might help wake me up. Tara insists that I am going for more walks than ever before. I think she may have been getting phone calls from my doctor who keeps stressing the need for more exercise.

Still, a walk in the brisk morning air doesn't seem to be doing much toward returning me to a full state of consciousness. It's clear it hasn't done much for Tara either. She usually spends the first hour or three after we return curled up asleep. Listening to her snoring under my desk seems to be sending me a subliminal message that I too should curl up on the floor and fall asleep with a rawhide chew in my mouth.

Whenever I think about needing to wake up so I can get on with my day, Neil Sedaka's voice starts running amok through my brain again. "Oh yes, waking up is hard to do..."

I never did like Neil Sedaka. Now I have him reminding me I'd rather be sleeping. I've been wracking my brain for a replacement song, but all I can come up with is Gordon Lightfoot singing, "I'm on my second cup of coffee and I still can't taste the day."

Actually, I'm on my fifth, and what I taste is telling me I should be buying a better brand of coffee.

These days I think it would take my second pot of coffee before I could even start thinking about how the day tastes. When you have a Labrador Retriever who likes to start her morning by licking your face, you really don't want to think about what the day tastes like.

That's reason enough to stick with Sedaka.

I always wake up at some point in the day. I'm usually at my most alert just as Jay Leno says goodnight. That might be part of the problem. My biological clock must have had a power failure, and I'm just not set right anymore. Somewhere deep inside me there is a little set of lights flashing 12:00, 12:00, 12:00...

I'm sure my wife would be glad to confirm that I'm not set quite right, but I think she's referring to my state of mind, not my state of consciousness.

The problem could also be dietary. Maybe I just need to start eating more energy boosting foods. Forget the salads. What kind of a jolt can a piece of lettuce or a slice of cucumber give you? I should be adding caffeine laden, energy boosting food groups to every meal.

Bring on the chocolate!

I Guess They Just Don't Serve My Kind There

Every few months my monosodium glutamate level drops to a dangerously low level and I need to go out for Chinese food. It doesn't have to be fancy. It doesn't have to have names I cannot pronounce. All I need is some chicken fried rice, sweet and sour chicken balls, and some beef in black bean sauce. A couple of egg rolls and a few fortune cookies complete the meal, and most importantly, none of the menu items I order contain noxious substances like broccoli.

I've always had a fear I may not be the most welcome patron at an all-you-can-eat Chinese buffet. When the owners see me coming, they always give me a look that seems to convey a fear on their part that I will be eating up their entire night's profits. OK, so I look like I could inhale the entire buffet and still feel a bit peckish, but that doesn't mean I will.

After all, I may want to save some room for dessert.

It doesn't even have to be a Chinese buffet to get those looks of fear. Several years ago I was part of a group of ten or twelve people that went to a moderately upscale steak house and buffet after an evening of other activities. The headwaiter was not sure he wanted to sit such a large group of people so close to closing time. He said he didn't have a table large enough for us.

The two largest people in the group were me and the late, great actor/comedian John Candy. Our shapes made people believe we could have been twin brothers of different mothers. John wasn't the sort of person you gave a hard time to at the door of a restaurant. He looked at the headwaiter and said, "Look. Just sit my friends here at a table, bring Gordon and I a couple of chairs to sit at the buffet, and be prepared to watch your financial situation get a whole lot worse before we're finished."

It was amazing just how fast a table became available for us. What wasn't quite as amazing was that it was as far from the buffet as we could possibly be seated in the restaurant without going into the alley out back.

My trip out for Chinese food the other night definitely left a sour taste in my mouth and it wasn't from the chicken balls, because we never got to the point of even ordering, much less consuming anything. We were asked to leave the restaurant before we could even get a glass of water.

It had nothing to do with my race, my religion, or even the fear of how much I might consume from the buffet. I don't have a reputation of starting brawls in the men's room of bars or restaurants. I don't start singing bawdy drinking songs while waiting for my meal, although in this particular restaurant it is apparently acceptable to stand up on a small stage and sing off-key renditions of Andy Williams' songs.

I will never listen to Moon River quite the same again.

There were plenty of tables available. In fact, only two other tables were occupied, which, considering it was a Friday night, probably should have told us something about the place.

The owner approached my wife at the table while I paid a visit to the restroom and said we would have to leave. It didn't even have anything to do with what I went to the restroom for. His reason was that he didn't want my assistance dog in his restaurant.

I can't imagine why. She's normally better behaved than I am.

I pointed out that the law clearly states "Refusal to provide equal access to people with disabilities accompanied by service dogs is a federal civil rights violation." Because of that fact Tara has been welcomed in restaurants, grocery stores, and theatres in Canada and the United States. Her favorite restaurant even makes sure she has a bottomless supply of peanut butter and a water dish when she stops in for a visit.

The owner of the restaurant may think he won because we left. I don't think so, because there is a rule of thumb in the restaurant business, "Make a customer happy and they'll tell three people. Make him unhappy and they'll tell ten."

The Kirkland codicil to that rule says, "Make Kirkland really ticked off and he'll write a newspaper column about it."

I Don't Need To Go Shopping For My Shortcomings

Shopping didn't used to fuel feelings of inadequacy. Twice in one day I was left reminded that certain things are beyond my capabilities.

Last weekend my wife wanted to look for a simple piece of furniture for her office. She suggested she could probably find it in just a few minutes in a furniture store near our home.

Oh, how wrong she was!

Not only that, but I was wrong, too, because I thought she was right. If it had been my idea we both would have known from the get go that it would be a big mistake, because as a husband, most of my ideas prove to be wrong one way or the other.

The problem arose when we assumed we could just spend a few minutes in any IKEA. Apparently the one they recently built near my house is the largest in the country. I wouldn't be surprised, because I think the thing covers three separate time zones. They should be running a helicopter service between the bedroom department and the dining room furniture.

One does not just run in and look for a bookcase in this store. I think there may still be a few people in there who attended the store's grand opening four years ago. They've been caught in a vortex that holds them spellbound rotating past futons, kitchen tables and entertainment units.

The sadistic Swede who designed the store has created a traffic flow that ensures no department will be missed. In order to get to the bookcases we had to take a route that started in sofas, cruised us passed kitchen cabinets, bedroom suites, and a compulsory pass by the in-store restaurant, just in case we took leave of our senses and decided to try the pickled herring.

Of course, I am giving you the English translation of all of this. There are no such things as futons, sofas, kitchen tables, or bedroom suites in an IKEA store. They all have names that sound like, "Ingerfingearaaaadno" and "Juumpinjimminy" which I believe is pronounced "Yumpinyimminy."

It's easy to get caught up in all of the excitement looking through the store. The furniture is displayed beautifully. It's almost enough to make you forget that, before it graces your home or office, it will fit in the trunk of your car with that special added feature:

Assembly required. So easy a child could assemble it.

OK, maybe a Swedish child with a doctorate in civil engineering, but not this particular Canadian who possesses all of the handyman skills of a musk ox. Our national animal here in the Great White North may be the ever-so-construction-oriented beaver, but that doesn't mean we all know how to create bookshelves with a stack of boards, a bag of hardware, and a twisted piece of metal that is supposed to tighten all the screws. Usually about halfway through the process I end up in the fetal position in a corner quietly crying for my mommy.

But I digress...

I'm not certain if we ever did find the bookcases. Returning to the car didn't mean we had successfully escaped the Swedish shopping vortex. The car's battery had died, which meant our shopping hadn't ended for the day after all.

The guy from the auto club suggested we replace the battery as soon as possible, preferably before we'd have to turn the car off again. We drove directly to an auto parts store, thinking it would be easy to get someone to put a new battery in the car. My aforementioned handyman skills aren't up for that chore, even though I'm almost certain I know where the battery is in the car.

OK, not a hundred percent certain, but almost.

I stayed in the car keeping it running while my wife went in to arrange for the new battery. The guy behind the counter offered to sell her a battery and lend her the tools to put it in herself. Diane is a very smart woman, despite what you might think is a shortcoming in the brains department for staying married to me for so many years. She can explain things like stocks and mutual funds, but changing a car battery is not in her repertoire either.

I think she probably explained that pretty clearly to the jerk behind the counter.

"Well," he said. "Is your car a 2.2 liter or a 2.4 liter?"

"It's blue," she said.

That's when she came out and told me we had to find another battery store.

It's also when I decided to stay away from stores for a while - at least until my self-esteem recovers, or a new one goes on sale someplace.

Gimme An R... Gimme An A... Gimme An I... Gimme and N

As I look out my office window, I see it is raining again. Of course it is. It's January and I live on the West Coast.

It's often said that it is easy to forecast the weather in this part of the world during the winter months. If you can't see the mountains, it means that it is raining. If you can see the mountains, it means it is going to rain soon.

The residents here don't tan; we rust.

This latest bout of rain started on December 18. There wasn't a rain-free day until January 14. For those of you who are counting, that's twenty seven days. The record for consecutive days of rain has stood since 1953. That year it rained for twenty-eight straight days.

We came so close to breaking the record, but it wasn't to be. The fifty-three year old record remains intact. The cycle of precipitation was broken.

As it was, it did rain at my house on the fifteenth, but it didn't rain at the airport where they take the official measurements. I live at the base of a mountain. If a cloud wanders past in an otherwise sunny day, it is going to drop rain when it hits the mountain. On an average year we get about sixty-seven inches of rain, while the airport only gets forty-four inches.

Any way you look at it, that's a lot of water. Thankfully, it doesn't all drop at once. I don't think my wife could tread water for long enough for the storm sewers to drain it away, and sixty-seven inches is over her head.

Thankfully, we don't see a lot of snow out here. If one inch of rain falls, it would equate to ten inches of snow. Can you imagine how long it would take to shovel six hundred and seventy inches of snow out of your driveway?

I think you might be late for work.

Of course, not too far up the mountain, it is coming down as snow. The ski resort at Mount Baker, about forty miles from my place, had to close the other day because eight feet of new snow fell in just four days. They actually had too much snow.

I think the avalanche rescue dogs probably refused to go outside. I know my dog would have.

Something that amazed me as more and more days of rain went by was that people actually started to hope we would break the record of twenty-eight consecutive days with measurable precipitation at the airport. Usually, at this time of year, any sight of the sun is greeted with awe.

We tend to forget what that bright yellow ball up in the sky is. And who made it blue up there instead of the gray we're used to?

Radio stations were flooded, not with water, but with callers asking if the record was still alive. It was almost as if people were cheering on the rain, as though it were some sort of Olympic athlete going for a record.

OK, so in the middle of January on the West Coast we don't have much to cheer about, but there has to be something more interesting than rain to keep people's attention.

They say every cloud has a silver lining. With all the clouds we've been seeing around here lately, it will be a wonder there was enough silver left for the second place medals at the next Olympics.

It's true, though. I ventured out into the back country below the snow line yesterday during the slight respite we got from the downpour and discovered the rain had brought about something the rest of you won't see for several months. Wildflowers have already started to bloom and trees are budding.

Nya nya nya-nya nya!

As I said, it's raining again as I look out my window. I can be pretty sure it will rain again tomorrow, and the next day, and the next.

And the next...

We've only got twenty-seven more days to go before we can break the record again. Go rain go!

Now, where did I put my snorkel?

Aiming For A Traveler's Sanctuary

Airports and airlines are always looking for ways to improve the experience of the traveling public. Some of their results are stupendous. Others seem a bit odd.

I spent the weekend in San Diego, starting of my 2006 appearance tour. This is the third consecutive year I have started in San Diego, because if I have to be somewhere in February, it's not going to be Fargo North Dakota or Churchill, Manitoba.

Because of a scheduling problem, I arrived at the Seattle airport with a few extra minutes to spare. To be precise, I had roughly five hundred and forty minutes to spare. On the way home, I had another spare four hundred and eighty minutes.

That's where the greatest invention ever came to my rescue.

The airline I use provides a lounge for travelers willing to pay a membership fee. One visit to the lounge left me with the impression that no fee would be too high for access to this sanctuary of travelers' bliss.

Out in the rest of the airport, harried travelers must share pre-boarding waiting areas with hundreds of other people, luggage carts, and small screaming children accompanied by large oblivious parents.

Long lines await any of them who feel the need for food or drink. When they finally get to the front of the line, they are met by food servers with questionable personal hygiene habits, and overly inflated prices for a food order that would take pocket change to pay for at any fast food drive-through.

Did I mention the screaming kids and the oblivious parents?

Once admission for to the lounge has been paid for, everything inside is free. That includes internet access, telephones, food, soft drinks, and an open and accommodating bar. That's right free beer, wine and liquor, all the necessary ingredients for a preflight relaxation regimen.

If you've ever experienced the alternative in an airport, I think you'll have to agree. It's The Greatest Invention Ever.

Of course, every silver lining must have its cloud, or in this case, clod.

The room was filled with business people, working on their laptop computers, sipping coffee, bloody Marys, wine and beer. A few were having quiet conversations on the telephones provided or on their wireless phones. Quiet, that is, except for the clod.

He talked into his telephone with a voice that reverberated throughout the room and out across the tarmac, through the forest and to all the ships at sea. We learned that he doesn't like his secretary, thinks his boss is a jerk, and wondered how he could deflect the blame for seriously annoying an important client.

It was clear that the rest of the people in the lounge were rapidly tiring of his loud litany and disgruntled diatribe. Perhaps he had been one of those screaming children of oblivious parents when he was younger.

It became clear who his employer was. Rude public behavior on the parts of its employees puts a company into a bad light. After listening to him for close to an hour, I know I'll avoid doing business with them in the future.

The next time I am in the market for a commercial jet, I won't be buying it from Boeing. That will teach them to let rude employees loose in otherwise pleasant surroundings.

As I mentioned above, there are also some strange new inventions making their presence known in and around airports. When I used a restroom, I saw a spiral, about the size of a quarter near the bottom of the urinals. I asked a janitor, who was cleaning the sinks, what they were or meant.

"They're urinal targets," he said; "A little something for people to aim at. It's made a huge difference to the amount of floor cleaning we have to do around the urinals. Apparently lot's of guys, who would normally be less than accurate, enjoy having a little mark to aim at."

I'm sure many of the people who were trying to work through the Boeing employee's long, loud telephone conversations would have preferred a little picture of his face, instead of the spiral.

I know I would.

When Healthy Eating Isn't

That will teach me.

I should have probably known, if I tried to do something that is supposed to be good for me, it would turn out badly.

And it did.

I could have gone for the tried and true, bad for me, unhealthy, trans fat laden burger. But no, I decided to be good and ordered the all white meat turkey wrapped in a healthy tortilla.

No all beef patties; no special sauce; no lettuce; no pickles. Not even a sesame seed bun. The only condiment that came with my sandwich was food poisoning.

Lots and lots of food poisoning.

I've had food poisoning before. It's always been a bit uncomfortable, and somewhat unpleasant. This went above and beyond uncomfortable, and was so far off the unpleasant scale that Webster's is going to have to rewrite the definition.

I didn't just think I was going to die. I wanted to die.

It would have been bad enough if it had happened around home. I could have been in my own bed. This happened on my way to the first weekend away my wife and I arranged in months. By the time the effects hit we were 450 miles from home, in a hotel room with a view of the ocean.

A hotel room we were paying a premium for in order to get that view of the ocean. The last thing I wanted to be thinking about was waves rising and crashing down on the beach. I had enough waves rising and crashing inside me.

So much for the walking along the beach, and the eating in small seaside bistros we had planned to celebrate getting through finishing my latest book and Diane surviving her busiest time of the year. So much for the drives along the coast to find secluded places only otherwise occupied by the occasional California sea lion. So much for any other activities that a couple might consider when away from home and live-in adult offspring, but that's another story.

Diane and the dog went on plenty of walks on the beach. She tried to tell me it was to get the dog some exercise, but I know the truth. She just didn't want to be there when either I died, or the next outpouring of the effects of food poisoning erupted.

It's probably best that I was in no condition to remember anything more complex than the route from the bed to the extremely small hotel bathroom. Had I had my wits about me, I might have remembered I was in Oregon, a state that has a physician-assisted suicide law on the books.

The pharmacist near the hotel sold Diane something for me to chew, which resembled the stuff I used to smack out of the blackboard erasers, when I was serving a detention in the seventh grade. She was also told to get me to drink those beverages football players pour over the heads of their coaches at the end of a winning game.

Now I know why they do that. It saves them from having to drink the stuff.

Naturally, when I got home I discovered that my own doctor was on vacation. He has a sixth sense about when I am going to need him for something unpleasant. I went to one of those walk-in clinics, where the doctor gave me marvelous advice.

"For the next couple of days get all your nutrition through liquid means," he said. "Whatever you want, as long as you can pour it."

Apparently, he was thinking along the lines of soup.

It should come as no surprise that soup is not the first liquid comes to mind when I want to drown my sorrows.

I may actually be onto something here. When you have food poisoning, you want to find a fast way to forget what is going on in your life, and you definitely do not want to remember it when it's over. Irish whiskey might just be the perfect medicinal compound to get you through the after-effects of a less than perfect supposedly good for you turkey sandwich.

It might not be a cure, but you won't care.

Believe me, though. Next time I'm going for the burger.

Fame Is Going To The Dogs

I'm losing my anonymity.

I mentioned a couple of weeks ago that the Canadian edition of Reader's Digest has a feature article about me in its April issue. All of a sudden, having seven million English Canadians and another two million French Canadians reading about me seems to have raised my visibility around here.

I've been writing this column for close to twelve years. I have four books on bookstore shelves, and I do a lot of radio and TV appearances, but I have managed to stay pretty anonymous around home.

I've often said that in our little town I am Mr. Diane Kirkland. Diane is a very successful stock broker, and she is involved in service clubs and foundations in our community. I've always just been that guy she is married to; the one nobody is really all that sure about.

"Well, we know he's married to Diane but we have no idea what he does," seems to be the general summation of my impact on the local community.

That's partially because, in those dozen years of writing the column, it has never appeared in the local media. It's always run in newspapers hundreds of miles from home. Most of the time, that's made my family pretty happy. My sons knew that, despite growing up through their teen years as characters in the column, their friends, and, more importantly, girlfriends' mothers were not going to read about them or their exploits. Diane could be almost certain her clients would not be reading about my take on marriage and the person I am married to.

Even so, Brad says he will probably end up talking to a therapist about growing up knowing everything he did could be the topic of one of his father's columns. Mike just keeps reminding me that he will be the one who picks the seniors' home I'll end up living in someday.

Even elsewhere in Canada, I have stayed more or less anonymous. The column has more readers in American newspapers than in my own country. I am often recognized in the streets in the United States, and sometimes it's even by people who don't think I am Michael Moore. Giving up wearing baseball caps helped a lot with that.

But that is all changing.

There is a great picture of Tara, my Labrador retriever assistance dog and me accompanying the Reader's Digest article. The photo shoot took place in a local coffee shop. Tara and I are at a table, both sitting in chairs, and she has her nose well into her coffee cup. The photographer took approximately 200 pictures that day. I could see the outline of the flash whenever I closed my eyes for the next two days. I thought I might have to get Tara a seeing-eye Chihuahua.

Ever since the magazine hit the stands, I've been receiving dozens emails each day from people who read the article. Because it was partially focused on how I came to be disabled, many of them have been offering me suggestions for cures.

I'm no doctor, but I'm pretty sure that the only thing crystals hung over my desk, magnets sewn into my bedding, and switching to an extreme vegan diet will do for me is decorate my office, make my bed uncomfortable, and increase my flatulence production.

And believe me, no one wants that.

Obviously, there are many people in the little town I live in who read Reader's Digest. I've been noticing people staring at me a bit more than usual in stores and restaurants. A few have actually waved or pointed at me.

Out of habit, I still check my fly whenever someone points at me. You just never know.

This morning, I knew that the article had really lifted the veil of anonymity here at home. Tara and I were out for a walk, when I saw a woman staring. After a moment, she approached us.

"Isn't that the dog that's in Reader's Digest this month?" she asked.

Wow. My stature has sure been lifted. No longer am I simply Mr. Diane Kirkland around here. Now, I'm the human companion of Tara, the Reader's Digest dog.

I've made it to the big time.

I'm Not Getting Older I'm Getting Distinguished

It seems like every time I look in the mirror, I see more salt than pepper.

When I get my hair cut, the floor of the shop is littered with gray under my chair. It used to be I could ask to have the gray ones cut out. If I did that today, I'd be almost bald, and I wouldn't want that. All things considered, I still think it's better to have hair that is having the opportunity to go gray, instead of the alternative.

I did a performance for a meeting of stock brokers last weekend. The wife of one of the younger brokers was heard saying how she thought her husband's little old gray haired clients were cute. Gray hair has absolutely nothing to do with qualifying for membership in the American Association of Retired Persons. I started to go gray in my mid-thirties.

Still, it's nice to be thought of as cute...

People close to me often make fun of the color my hair has turned. My wife has just a couple of gray hairs appearing in her dark brunette coiffure. I have often said that it is proof of which one of us is easier to live with, but she disputes that fact for some reason or another. I can't understand her position, because, after all, it's been well documented.

I am a freaking saint.

The fact that I am the one doing the documenting is beside the point.

She points out I look so much older than she does, when we all know that she is considerably older than I am. OK, so it's only five and a half months but in my mind that is a considerable amount of time, and I'd like you all to just go along with me on that.

Even my doctor seemed to be commenting on it. Every time I went to see him he would suggest that I dye it. It turns out he was recommending that I diet. Neither of which are particularly appealing.

Red hair runs in my family. When I started to go gray, it was the red highlights in my hair and beard that changed color first. I do not remember my father with red hair. He was in his forties when I was born, so as far back as I can remember him, his hair was already gray.

At the time I thought it was odd that my beard started to go gray well ahead of the hair on my head. After all, my beard is about sixteen years younger than my hair.

There are, of course, many men who would prefer to dye their hair than face the fact they've gone gray. Personally, I cannot understand that urge, especially when the results look so unnatural. It may work for some hair colors, but not for red hair. Instead of the desired result of looking younger, the men who use those products usually end up just looking ridiculous.

A friend of mine was a radio and television personality, who tried to return to his youthful carrot red hair. It was a futile attempt to maintain the young look he felt he needed in the business. He bought the name brand hair color for men. The result was not pretty. Every single strand of hair ended up exactly the same color as the one beside it. There were no highlights of other hair colors to soften the impact. He looked like he had been attacked by a spray can wielding mugger who opened fire and inflicted a severe carrot red head wound.

You could see him coming from three blocks away.

His head looked like an orange felt-tip marker that had been left sitting with its cap off for too long. It had the same effect as a massive car accident. You didn't want to look at it, but you could help but stare in wonder.

Women often complain that gray hair makes men look distinguished, and women look old. If that's the case, I am getting more and more distinguished every day. If this keeps up I will be the most distinguished person on the planet. Even my chest, and my ... uhm... you know... are becoming distinguished.

Who could ask for more?

I Try To Avoid Cows In Heat

I think Al Gore might be right.

The Earth is definitely getting warmer. At least it is around my house. Part of the attraction of living in the Pacific Northwest is that most of the year the temperature stays within a fairly narrow range. We still get four distinct seasons, except ours are spring, fall, a Tuesday in July, and Thursday in January.

We're having a long, hot Tuesday this year.

I just hope that doesn't mean we're going to be in for a hard Thursday in January.

Knowing that it never gets too hot around here, we did something a couple of weeks ago that, in retrospect, might not have been a good idea without checking the long range weather forecast.

We arranged to have our carpets cleaned.

Adding several gallons of water to the carpets in the middle of a long hot Tuesday is not a good idea. All that water needs evaporate, making it clear to my son who has spent almost all of his life in this temperate climate what people mean when they say, "It isn't the heat. It's the humidity."

Ever since the carpet cleaners left, we've been dealing with both.

It became so uncomfortable, I had lapse in my normal mediocre degree of common sense. It forced me to agree that it might be a good idea to go and do something I would normally never consider.

I said I'd accompany my wife on a visit to a cow barn, partially because it sounded like it might not be as hot and humid as our apartment. As it turned out, it wasn't.

With the exception of horses, I am not a big fan of barnyard animals. Cows, in particular, are not high on my list of critters I feel any special affinity toward – even when they are calves. I guess that's partially a throwback to the scare I got as a kid, when I tried to take a shortcut through a field that was home to a rather large, and - as it turned out - fast running bull.

I've always believed that, given the opportunity, a cow would just as soon step on your shoes as poop on them. Luckily, I don't have a lot of feeling in my feet so the former is not as much of a problem anymore, but if a cow poops on your shoe, no matter how severe a paraplegic you are, you are still going to have the same reaction.

Normally, that involves reciting a list of words including one in particular that actually defines what landed on your shoe.

Diane and I headed out to our local fair with the main intent of visiting the dairy cattle exhibit. For the first few minutes, the barn smelled exactly like I expected it to. After that, my hay fever kicked in and I couldn't smell anything. I wasn't sure if I was sorry or thankful I had forgotten to take an antihistamine before going to the fair.

Had it not been for a good cause, I never would have put myself in that situation. My wife sponsors the local 4H club's dairy calf entrants. We were there to see the calves the kids were showing.

I have a hard time saying no to things that help kids keep occupied on positive activities, and 4H certainly fits that bill. Without that organization, we'd probably see a lot more young people turning away from farming as a way of life. That could have a detrimental effect on my supply of hamburgers, cheese, bacon and other necessary crops.

I have to admit, the calves the kids were showing looked nothing like any of the cattle I have seen in other barns. These calves had been pampered, washed, and blow-dried. I've been to many a car wash, but that was definitely the first time I had ever seen a drive-through cow wash. They were brushed and primed, looking more like large dogs than the sad-eyed cows I have seen in beef feedlots.

As I looked at the kids working on their calves, I was struck by one thought: thank goodness the local 4H club didn't offer programs to encourage its members to raise broccoli.

I Have A Point

In a few days it will be the twelfth anniversary of the first *Gordon Kirkland At Large* column. Perhaps this is a good time to apologize to my readers.

Again.

A few weeks ago, I referred to the amount of room on my computer's hard drive as memory. Apparently, that was wrong and I am so very sorry.

I have never claimed to be anything in the way of a computer expert. My computer is a tool I use to write the column, my books, and my comedy material. I couldn't care less about how it does its job, just as long as it keeps doing it.

For the most part, my computer does that job quite nicely and without complaint, which is more than I can say for my staff when I was a federal government employee many years ago. Those people were like the cannons you see at battlefield memorials.

They didn't work and you couldn't fire them.

Somewhere inside the computer is a hard drive that remembers everything I have written for the last twelve years. In my mind, when you remember something it involves memory.

According to the readers who wrote to chastise me for saying that, I should have been calling it my hard drive storage capacity. To do otherwise is something that makes the supergeeks out there nauseous.

I did a little research, so that I would not offend them so egregiously again in the future. I found a website that explained the difference between memory and storage. It said the hard drive may also be called "Storage" or "Disk Space" and it is measured in Megabytes. Memory is also called "RAM" and it is measured in Megabytes.

Boy that sure cleared that up, didn't it?

I also have to apologize to all of those British people who are not English, or is it all those English people who are not British?

I interchanged the terms British and English in a recent column. Apparently, Scots don't like it when you do that. From the mail I received it is clear that, if they actually wore underwear under their kilts, it would get into quite a tight knot every time someone lumps them together with the people of England.

I can't even print some of the comments I received from the Scottish soccer fans, who were upset when I categorized all British soccer fans with English soccer fans.

Some of those people need their mouths washed out with haggis.

From the gist of their letters, I gather that Scottish soccer fans are all genteel and polite, while English soccer fans are the ones prone to rioting. I received several emails pointing out that Glasgow's Celtic Football Club received a special award from FIFA for their fans polite behavior.

That's probably enough to set Robert the Bruce or Bonnie Prince Charlie spinning in their graves. I don't think they gave out politeness awards at the Battles of Bannockburn or Culloden.

I'm always a bit amused by the people who take what I write just a little too seriously. I am not a news reporter. I write about the absurdities of life, and frankly, it doesn't get much more absurd than a bunch of geeks worrying about whether I call it memory or hard disk storage capacity.

A few years ago, I received complaint letters concerning the column I wrote about having a colonoscopy. Apparently, some people were afraid I might discourage others from having the procedure. Let's face it. If you are going to take your medical advice from a humor column in a newspaper, then you are probably doing the gene pool a favor by not having potentially life-saving diagnostic procedures.

To settle down my critics on that issue, let me say once and for all, that I was only kidding when I said they shoved a tripod up my colon to steady the camera they were inserting.

It only felt that way.

I have a t-shirt with a quote from Kingsley Amis, the British, or I guess I should say English, poet and novelist. He sums it all up quite nicely.

"If you can't annoy someone, there is no point in writing."

Amen to that.

In The Early Morning Purple Rain

There are some advantages and disadvantages to living on the edge of the city. Our neighborhood is partially residential and partially agricultural. Being close to farmland is important to me. I grew up in a small town north of Toronto, Ontario and have always enjoyed the sights and sounds of farm country.

The smells are another story, but we'll ignore them for now.

There are two main cash crops around here; three if you count the illegal one. Our little community produces a huge percentage of the North American cranberry crop in the marshes and bogs, and blueberries on the drier land. It's great to be able to go and get either of those crops fresh from the fields.

In all the years I have been living here, I hadn't encountered a disadvantage to living close to those crops. In fact, I wasn't even aware of one until last week. I suppose, if I had thought about it, I might have been able to foresee the situation, but it just never crossed my mind.

In every blueberry field around here there is a devise that sets off a small explosion every couple of minutes to scare the birds away from the crop. At this time of year, when blueberries are at the peak of their production, it can sound like we are living somewhere on the outskirts of Baghdad or in southern Lebanon.

The explosions may startle the birds and make them take flight, but they just circle around and return for a quick blueberry fix before the gun fires again. Huge flocks of blackbirds spend their summer vacations in our community.

I'm sure I will here from some ornithological group telling me I should not be calling them blackbirds. They may be starlings or grackles, or cowbirds, but they are birds and they are black so I will call them blackbirds.

I added a certain adjective to the name last week, but it cannot be used in a mainstream newspaper.

I was sitting at a red light, when I saw a huge flock of blackbirds rise up from a blueberry field, like lawyers in a Dick Cheney hunting party. Without exaggeration there must have been well over one hundred birds in the flock. They circled over the road ahead of me and then started heading back to the blueberry field. Their flight path took them directly over my car.

It was a clear day, but despite the lack of clouds, a storm suddenly erupted. I could see it hitting the road ahead, and could hear it hitting my car like hailstones. I was suddenly reminded of the movie starring the artist formerly known as Prince.

This was no summer shower. It was purple rain.

Apparently, blueberries go through blackbirds without stopping along the way for much of a color change.

It was shock and awe in a less destructive, but equally shocking and awing sense. I was thankful my sunroof was closed, because it took several direct hits, as did my windshield, hood and roof.

I stopped for gas a little while later in my polka-dotted car. The man beside me at the pumps was wearing the colors of a well known motorcycle club generally noted for the toughness of its members.

"You'd better watch out for a new hazard on the road for motorcyclists," I said, pointing to the large purple blotches on my car. "Those blueberry eating blackbirds are bombing the highway."

"Oh, gross," he said. "Can you imagine driving through that on a bike?"

The man, who would probably face a knife-wielding opponent in a bar fight without so much as batting an eye, was clearly shaken by the thought of getting hit in the helmet by second-hand blueberries. As he drove off, I saw him hunch down a bit and scan the sky before pulling out onto the highway.

My mother always used to say it was good luck to be crapped on by a bird. She explained her reasoning when I came home one day with a large white stain on the arm of my shirt. She figured that no matter what, if a bird drops a bomb on you, you luck just has to get better.

It couldn't get worse.

Singing Or Something Resembling It

I made my singing debut last weekend. That should be enough to scare even those who claim to be open-minded music listeners. You may be partial to jazz, rap, heavy metal, classic rock and/or country, but I'm not sure you are quite prepared for Kirkland.

Almost a year ago, I was asked to develop a show to be presented at the Watermark Writer's Conference at a resort in western Washington State. I called my friend, singer-songwriter Greg Greenway, It's been said Greg has *"one of the strongest, and finest voices in folk music."* Boston Globe says, *"Confessional one moment, rambunctiously disarming the next, few modern folk singers can own a coffeehouse stage as completely as Greenway."*

Greg's songwriting ability is incredible. He takes his audience through a roller coaster ride of emotional responses to his words; one moment laughing, and the next moved almost to the point of tears.

Basically, Greg is to music what I am not.

We decided to write what we began calling a folk-rock opera, detailing every phase of a writer's career in song.

Greg and I were faced with one rather significant obstacle that none of the great songwriting duos have had to deal with in their careers. The Gershwins could sit together in a room and churn out their songs. I live near Vancouver, British Columbia. Greg is just around the corner and a short 3300 miles further down the road on Cape Cod in Massachusetts. It doesn't exactly lend itself to getting together for an afternoon of songwriting.

Despite that, after many attempts to single-handedly revitalize the financial condition of the North American telephone industry, including one lengthy call while Greg drove across Ohio and Western Pennsylvania between concerts, we managed to write eighteen songs.

We still desperately needed rehearsal time. We arrived at the resort two days before the show. Greg flew cross-country from Boston to get to the resort and I drove the couple hundred miles from mile place. Thanks to construction and hitting Seattle just in time for the start of rush hour, I think I was in transit longer than he was.

It turned out we would not have a piano for Greg at the resort until just before we took to the stage. Hearing of our plight, one of the resort employees offered us the use of her home, which conveniently included a fully equipped recording studio.

I've visited a number of recording studios over the years. They usually have some form of insulation covering the walls to absorb the sound. Often it looks like a collection of egg cartons covering the walls. This studio also had a collection covering the walls to deaden the sound and prevent echoing.

I counted well over 60 pieces of taxidermy, ranging in size from a fish head to a fully grown black bear standing erect on his hind legs. Around the room were deer, elk, lynx, cougar, moose, a buffalo, and more. One black bear head had antlers growing from it, making it look like the issue of some kind of backwoods interspecies sexual encounter.

It was a bit unnerving having over one hundred and thirty eyes staring down on us while we rehearsed.

We started out with a song about someone wanting to become a writer, and moved through other steps in the career ranging from desperation to see work published, getting that first big break, and on to the joys of book tours and being stalked by a deranged fan.

One song, more of a medley of songs, looked at all of the various genres someone could write in for publication. We covered the romance novel, the psycho-thriller and the cowboy western. In a line that Greg and I are particularly proud of, we gave some serious advice to anyone wanting to write science fiction, when we sang, "Never end a fantasy with a cyborg and a Wookie. It's an ugly, scaly, oily, hairy mess."

I'm happy to tell you that the lyrics and Greg's singing were a hit in front of our audience of writers who had either experienced the phases of the career we were singing about or were hoping to in the near future.

My singing... well, that's another story.

Dog Days In Home Improvement Store

As I have often written, I 'walk' with a combination of crutches clipped to my forearms and the assistance of my service dog, Tara.

Most people are familiar with seeing-eye dogs for the blind, but the other roles dogs take on for people with special needs are less well known. There are dogs for people who are deaf, paraplegics and quadriplegics, and several other situations. There are even dogs that can predict and warn their human partners of an impending epileptic seizure.

Tara picks up anything I drop so that I don't have to bend over. Sometimes if I start to bend over, I keep going until I am flat on my face on the floor. Some people find that quite entertaining.

She can also open a door or push an elevator call button if my hands are full. Her most important job is to brace her body against mine to give me extra stability. A side benefit of it all is that she has forced me to get more exercise than I might otherwise, because I have not been able to train her to use the toilet. Without that exercise, I would have been back in the wheelchair by now.

Tara goes pretty well everywhere with me, although there is one local grocery store that we now avoid after that nasty wagging tail meet's stacked display of cereal boxes incident.

The restaurants we frequent are quite used to Tara. They know she isn't going to scream and squeal at the top of her lungs like so many of the small children brought into restaurants by parents who think that is cute behavior.

"Oh, look. Little Stephanie just made that man spill his coffee into his lap when she hit that high pitch. Isn't that sweet?"

For that matter, the restaurant staff knows Tara is better behaved than me.

Those of you who have been reading this column for several years will remember Tara's predecessor. Nipper, the dumbest dog to ever get lost on a single flight of stairs, was a loyal and loving cocker spaniel, who had the cerebral abilities of a sack full of rusty nails. I would never have thought to take Nipper to a store or restaurant.

There has been an unfortunate fad developing over the past couple of years. A couple of dumb and dumber actress/singer/celebrities who have overused their fifteen minutes of fame started carrying around small dogs wherever they go. As a result, dumb and dumber actress/singer/celebrity wannabees have been carrying small dogs with them wherever they go.

I've had to stop shopping at a certain large home improvement chain's stores, because they have opened their doors to every person who wants to bring a dog along to help them pick out paint colors. (If I mention the store by name, the advertising departments at newspapers carrying this column will run to the editors and complain that I am insulting their hyper-sensitive customers... again. Let's just say that if you have a home, it's probably a depot you've visited.)

Every time Tara and I have been in one of their stores lately, we have had to deal with some irresponsible dog owner. Women carrying yappy little Yorkshire Terriers, and men leading their Chihuahuas on expandable leashes seem to be everywhere in the store. I've even seen one lift its leg against a pile of lumber. One woman, whose dachshund came running up to us, told me she thought my dog would like some company.

Tara thought she might like a wiener dog on a bun; perhaps with a bit of mustard and relish.

The woman seemed rather nonplussed when Tara let her dietary desires be known in a rather vocal way. Actually, she was just telling the other dog to stay away from my feet, because she didn't want to have to help me back up if I tripped over it.

I did enjoy the sight of the woman who was carrying her small dog pressed tightly into her more than ample bosom. The dog was dressed in a sweater that matched the one the owner was wearing. The dog stared at me with a look that was immediately translatable.

"For the love of God, please... call the SPCA."

It's Not Raining, It Pouring

"Water, water everywhere and not a drop to drink."

Never have those words rung truer than around my place for the past few days. OK. I live in the Pacific Northwest, and should be used to seeing rain beginning in October and easing up sometime in May, but this is ridiculous.

In the first three weeks of the month, we have had more rain than we did in the previous six months combined. On one rather spectacular day we saw nearly five inches of rain.

I think one of my neighbors is building an ark.

Parts of the city have been without electricity since the storm blew through. Along with the rain, we had winds strong enough to topple huge trees.

It was nothing on the scale of Katrina. Robin Williams won't be gathering his friends to hold a benefit for the area. Sean Penn won't be cruising around in his boat looking for stranded residents. Still, for the poor guy who now has five large cedar trees impaled in his roof, it was a disastrous storm.

An ironic result of that storm was that, despite the deluge of pure water falling from the sky, we no longer have drinkable water flowing from our taps. The rain and wind caused landslides to cascade into the city's water reservoirs, leaving the water flowing from the taps looking like something you would normally flush down the toilet.

Let's face it. This has been weather that isn't fit for man or beast. My assistance dog looks out the door, and gives me a look that clearly communicates her thoughts.

"Uh... Gord... How be we just forget about it, and I'll hold it until it stops raining?"

Not that I am particularly opposed to that idea, but after a day or so, I think she would probably make a sloshing sound when she walks.

It only goes to show that Tara is smarter than many of the people who live around here. They are so environmentally disturbed that they will head out into the forest in a torrential rainstorm. Unfortunately, around here, heading out into the woods is quickly followed by climbing into the mountains. It doesn't rain so much in the mountains at this time of year. It comes down as that stuff those of you in less temperate parts of the country shovel out of your driveways.

Search and rescue teams recently had to risk their own safety to head out into the back country, looking for a man they had previously rescued a month earlier. It was the third time they had to go after this same individual. According to news reports they are beginning to lose patience with him.

Ya think?

It's one thing to get lost in the woods. It's quite another to set out at this time of year wearing nothing but light slacks and a t-shirt. At least he got a new word added to his vocabulary.

Hypothermia.

In another recent case, searchers were able to find a missing man when they spotted the light from his I-pod. Forget warm clothes. Forget proper footwear. Forget staying on marked trails. But never, ever forget to bring your tunes when you go into the woods.

Had those five inches of rain we had the other day fallen as snow, we would have been buried under over four feet of white stuff. If there can be any certainties about living in this region, one that is very real is the fact that people from the northwest and snow do not happily coexist.

I have often told the story of watching a man skid sideways down a hill after a couple of inches of snow fell. His knuckles were white as they gripped his steering wheel and his eyes were as wide as Tweety Bird's.

He was driving the sand and salt spreading truck.

At least in rain we don't need sand or salt. We don't have to shovel it. We don't need to dodge other drivers who do not know how to handle their cars or trucks on snowy roads.

We just have to make sure we know how to tread water.

I'm Losing My Inherited Company Loyalty

My father was a company man.

He graduated from high school at the height of the Depression, and was faced with a decision. He could continue to teach swimming for ten dollars a week, or go to work for General Electric for nine. Knowing that swimming instruction was not a long term career choice, but being resourceful, he rescheduled his lessons, took the nine dollars a week from GE and kept earning the ten from his swimming students.

He and my mother planned to be married when he was making twenty dollars a week. They didn't wait that long.

Dad was fiercely loyal to General Electric. Other job offers came over the years, but he stuck it out through thirty-nine-and-a-half years. He retired six months short of earning a forty-year gold watch, but said he had reached the point where he didn't really care what time it was. In his eyes, the company had been loyal to him, giving him a paycheck every two weeks, and keeping his job waiting for him when the Second World War called him away. He owed them loyalty in return.

Our house was a General Electric house. There wasn't as much as a light bulb that wasn't made in one of the company's plants. From toasters to refrigerators and from televisions to dishwashers, everywhere you looked you could see the GE logo.

When children are born, they are often given the names of relatives. My brother was named for our only uncle. I was named for the company. My first and middle names, Gordon and Edward, gave me the initials GE.

I advertize for the company Thomas Edison founded every time I sign my name.

The names of other appliance companies were almost blasphemous in our house. We all knew mentioning Westinghouse or Sylvania in my father's presence was as bad as, if not worse than, the more classic forms of cursing.

Over the years, I've also bought a lot of GE products. It isn't out of any sense of loyalty to my father's old employer. It's more a feeling of guilt that comes over me if I consider buying a light bulb made by someone else. Even though my father passed away twenty-five years ago, I still feel like I'm letting him down if I consider another brand of toaster.

When we moved, the buyer of our old place wanted our freezer included in the deal. We let her have it. It was fifteen years old, and bound to need replacing soon anyway. We looked at two freezers. I could hear my father's voice admonishing me to pick the GE.

Not wanting to cause him to roll in his grave, we ordered the GE, but I think he may be doing a few rotations when we go out to replace the dishwasher and stove later this month.

It has nothing to do with the quality of GE's products. It's the quality of service from the company they subcontract with to make their deliveries.

We received a call saying the freezer would be delivered sometime on December twenty-third. Wonderful. We didn't have anything else to do on the Saturday before Christmas, so why not sit at home waiting for a truck? Part way into the morning, we received another call saying it would not be delivered that day. We'd have to wait until the following Thursday.

Thursday morning came and went. Mid-afternoon, I called the delivery company and was told we were not on their scheduled delivery list for that day. Apparently, I should have known this because they hadn't called to confirm the day before, even though they had confirmed five days earlier. I asked if I should have used ESP or read tea leaves to know I was wasting my time.

It took another two days for the truck to arrive in our driveway. You might think that we are now cheerfully keeping food frozen in our shiny new GE freezer. Unfortunately, the space we set aside for it remains empty. The one they tried to deliver was so badly dented, I wouldn't take it. Whatever they'd stacked on top of it in the truck crushed the lid.

I told them they could shove it up their Westinghouse and to Frigidaire off.

...And They Want Me As A Member?

I think it was Groucho Marx who once said, "I would never want to belong to a club that would have me as a member."

A couple of days ago a large envelope arrived in my mailbox that bore the words, "Your membership has been approved." Inside there was a credit card style membership card, a decal, and two metal zipper pulls shaped like the club logo so that other members could identify me by looking at my zipper.

I'm not all together certain about joining a club that lets its members identify one another that way.

I want to make it clear that I have nothing against the people who share the lifestyle as members of this particular club. I even have some very good friends who are like that. I'm just not one of them. I know there are those who would keep their indulgence in this sort of thing to themselves. There are others who want to shout it out and flaunt it to the world, so I guess belonging to this club might be attractive to them. I have to give those in the second group a certain amount of credit, because there are vocal individuals and organizations that are opposed to that sort of lifestyle.

I suppose clubs like this are a natural progression. This activity has been around since prehistoric times, but it gets so much publicity these days. There are even television shows dedicated to making it seem like a perfectly natural pastime.

By now I'm sure you will have realized I am talking about fishing.

The letter that came in the package from the North American Fishing Club stated, "From what we know about you, you are our kind of fisherman."

If that's the case, their kind of fisherman is a guy who hasn't had a rod in his hands for over five years, could count the number of times he's been fishing in the last twenty-five years on one hand, and who would define a good day of fishing as one that he didn't catch anything because that meant he didn't have to clean and gut a bunch of dead fish.

After detailing all of the different aspects of club membership the author of the letter said, "I'm sure you understand why we can't let half-hearted fishermen have access to the club's benefits."

I used to do a lot of fishing as a kid. We had a summer cottage north of Toronto. Our boat only had a 7-horsepower motor, so water skiing was eliminated from our list of activities. That left us swimming, sitting beside the lake throwing rocks into the water, and fishing. Since our mother followed the rule about waiting an hour after eating to go swimming, and throwing rocks into the water didn't have that great an appeal, we had at least three hours each day to spend fishing.

The letter went on to say that the club is for the outdoorsman who fishes smart. "Fishing smart" to me means putting the bait on the hook without impaling my finger.

I'd consider myself a smart fisherman on any day I went fishing without forgetting to bring a cooler full of beer to give myself something to do, because my likelihood of catching anything is somewhere between slim and none – leaning more towards the none than the slim.

I will admit to lingering on a couple of those fishing shows on TV a few times when I've been channel flicking. I guess it's those guys this club is really aimed at attracting. You see them pulling in huge bass, trout, and walleye. They're the kind of fish you see mounted on wooden plaques over fireplaces in lodges and sporting goods stores. What I can't understand is that these supposedly smart fishermen have never heard of a hammer. Instead of knocking the fish senseless and throwing them into a cooler at the back of the boat, they do the absolute unthinkable in the minds of those of us who have never caught anything remotely that size.

They throw them back.

Just the other day I saw a guy bring in a sailfish that had to weigh two hundred pounds. After fighting with it for a couple hours he got into the boat, looked at it for a minute, and threw it back.

If I ever got myself invited on one of those shows and actually caught something like a two hundred pound sailfish that took two hours to bring to the boat, they'd have to hit me on the head with a hammer before they could throw it back.

Give a man a fish and he'll eat for a day. Teach him how to fish smart and he'll get a TV show so he doesn't have to eat fish anymore.

What Am I Offered For A Slightly Used Self Esteem?

I broke a longstanding vow last weekend. It's one of those things I know I shouldn't do. I've done it a few times in the past, all with equally bad results. I swore I wouldn't do it again. Several people who saw me doing it reminded me that I had made that vow, and they seemed somewhat bemused to see me breaking it. I suppose I could take solace in the fact that I am not entirely to blame for my indiscretion. Just like Adam with the apple, I have an excuse -- my wife made me do it.

We had a garage sale.

We're moving next weekend. A lot of stuff that has accumulated over the years in this place that we really see no need to pay movers $85.00 per hour to cart to the new one. Somehow, the idea of holding a garage sale was slipped into my subconscious, where it festered into reality.

Just in case you might have missed my point, I hate garage sales. I hate just about everything about them. It takes a whole day to get ready for them; it takes another day to recover from them; and, worst of all, it takes a whole day sitting in the driveway putting up with people offering you a quarter of the price you're asking for an item that you know cost you ten times as much when you bought it just last year.

Perhaps, if I had better luck with garage sales in the past, I might not be so much against having one again. My garage sale luck hasn't just been bad. It's been abysmal. This was probably the fifth time in my life that I have swallowed any semblance of self-pride and loaded a bunch of stuff into the driveway. It's only the second time we have not awoken to torrential rain on the appointed day.

One past garage sale deserves special mention. It was probably one of the greatest disasters in recent garage sale history. Remember the saying in the Sixties that was something like "suppose they gave a war and nobody came?" We are probably the only people who ever gave a garage sale and nobody came -- not even my wife, although I still say she somehow arranged to be called in to work that Saturday.

We thought we did everything right. We posted signs at the end of our street. We ran ads in the local community newspapers. We wrote out price tags for every item, and organized them in groups of similar items. We had everything set up an hour before we were scheduled to start, and my sons and I sat in the driveway waiting for the hoards of bargain hunters to descend on us like a plague of locusts.

...and we waited...

...and waited...

After a while, the boys got bored and retreated to the important business of destroying evil villains on their video games.

The street was deathly quiet. We were still fairly new in the area, so at first the quietness of the street didn't seem too out of place. Finally, after several hours, my curiosity got the better of me and I walked to the end of our driveway. It was instantly clear why we were void of all customer activity. The police had the end of our street cordoned off. No one could get in or out. Even if I decided to set fire to everything in the driveway, the fire department couldn't have dropped by for a visit.

All their trucks were busy leading the parade that was passing by the end of our street.

That's when I learned that there is an annual parade along the two main thoroughfares through town. No one in their right mind would schedule a garage sale to coincide with the all the side streets being blocked off to facilitate the event.

That was also the day I made the vow about never hosting another garage sale. After last weekend I am going to renew my vow. I'm not sure what is more encouraging to someone trying to quell the urge to sell stuff in his or her driveway. If it's not having anyone show up to buy your junk, it's definitely got to be having a couple of hundred people from the shallow end of the gene pool show up wanting to barter over the value of a plastic storage container that's missing it's lid. That, plus the roving bands of pre-adolescents who repeatedly ask if there is anything they can buy for a nickel.

Sure kid. That's about what my self-esteem is worth right now.

Bad Canadian... No Bacon, Beer, Or Donuts For Me

I have to admit I feel a little bit guilty when I look out my window today. I guess living like this makes me a bad Canadian.

I'm writing this column in February. Outside it looks like May. There isn't a cloud in the sky. Leaves are starting to appear on the trees. Flowers are blooming. People are walking around without parkas, gloves, toques, earmuffs, or frostbite.

And I'm still in Canada.

February days like this are obviously part of the reason Vancouver was just named one of the most livable cities in the world. In a survey conducted by the William M. Mercer Company to help their clients determine if employees stationed in various cities around the world deserved hardship bonuses, we were tied with Zurich.

That's Zurich, Switzerland, not the Zurich in Ontario, Montana, or California.

I watch the weather reports on TV, I've seen the way the rest of my countrymen, along with most of the people in the United States who live north of the Mason-Dixon Line are suffering. St. John's Newfoundland is buried under fifteen feet of snow or more. Buffalo, New York isn't much better off.

I feel so badly for the people living in those places I try not to laugh. No, really; honest; I do.

I received a note from my much older sister the other day. She said, "I really need you not to tell me about the forsythia and crocuses that must be blooming out there. This has been one mother of a winter here and if it ever happens again, I'm going to quit. The sun did come out this afternoon but unfortunately I was picking a pencil up from under my desk and I missed it."

Naturally, I did what any much younger brother would do upon reading that. I returned her note with descriptions of the flowers blooming outside. I abided by her request though. I didn't mention the forsythia or the crocuses, just the daffodils, tulips and pansies. I'm still waiting for a response, but I'm almost certain it won't be printable in a mainstream newspaper.

It's not like we haven't had to put up with a certain amount of hardship out here this winter. I've heard reports on a couple of mornings the frost was so heavy people have been forced to spend a full fifteen seconds scraping it off their windshields. I realize it sounds hard to believe and I can't confirm it because I've never actually witnessed it myself. I know one guy who claims he's already ruined three credit cards this year trying to clear off his windshield. Going out the next morning to find that frost has once again formed on the windshield gives those of us in one of the world's most livable cities an idea what you people are going through when you finish shoveling out your driveway in time for the snowplow to fill it in again.

Frustrating isn't it?

We did have one horrific snowstorm just before Christmas. Almost four inches of snow hit the ground overnight, and it took until almost 10:00 in the morning for it all to melt. Thankfully it was a Saturday and I slept in until 9:00, so I only suffered through the cabin fever caused by being trapped inside due to the snow for an hour. I couldn't have handled much more

I really do have to admit that this has been an unusually pleasant winter out here. Usually by this point in the year the schools have had to close three or four times due to a heavy snowfall. Of course our definition of a heavy, school-closing blizzard is probably a bit different from the rest of the world. Kids out here don't get a snow day unless there is at least a half an inch of snow on the ground. After all we don't want to molly-coddle them.

Like I said at the outset, my good fortune to live here makes me feel a little bit guilty when I think about the hardships so many faced this winter. Look on the bright side though. If you're in New York, you're still in the top half of the list. Torontonians can almost feel proud to be tied with Tokyo and Montreal for nineteenth place. Los Angeles and Paris tied for thirty-third place, just ahead of Seattle (35th), London (40th), and Brazzaville, Republic of Congo (215th).

Face it. It could be a lot worse. You might be knee-deep in fresh snow after the latest snowstorm, but you're better off than people in Baghdad. It placed 211th. You just have snow dropping from the sky.

It doesn't hurt nearly as much as a rocket propelled grenade or the back half of a Volkswagen somebody used as a car bomb.

I'm Not Qualified To Shop In Big Hardware Stores

They opened one of those hardware stores with an overactive thyroid near me the other day. Personally I found the whole experience confusing.

OK, I've admitted it before; I am not even close to anyone's description of handy. My greatest desire when pounding a nail is that I actually hit the metal nail and not one of the nails made from my cells. I do not own any power tools. I did once, but that was many years ago, when I was young, reckless, and stupid about things like that. Now that I am older and wiser, I can accept that power tools can inflict a lot more damage on me than I could ever inflict on a piece of wood. I tried a chainsaw once, and would just rather not think about that experience if you don't mind.

My father could have really gotten excited about a store like that. Some people remember their driving vacations because of the scenic or historic sites they might have visited along the way. My father set his standard for vacation quality based solely on the size of the hardware stores he visited.

My wife and I dropped by the grand opening of this new megastore of injury and death waiting to happen. Naturally, I was confused.

It wasn't the four hundred different kinds of light bulbs they stocked that bewildered me. I can accept there are probably people out there who could name the proper use for each one. They may not have what you and I might call a life, but they could identify all those light bulbs.

I wasn't even confused to see there were people actually buying the materials to rewire their houses. Personally the closest I am willing to get to electrical repairs is checking to see if the coffeepot is plugged in before I hit its switch in the morning. I feel pretty much the same way about plumbing supplies. My plumbing ability is largely limited to jiggling the handle on the toilet. If the kitchen tap is dripping I will try jiggling the handle on the toilet. If a geyser is erupting behind the washing machine, I'll try jiggling the handle on the toilet. If that fails it is a sure sign it is time to call someone who knows what they are doing.

They have one entire aisle dedicated to screws. Why? In my experience there are only three types of screws. There are the ones that aren't fat enough to fill the hole you're trying to put it into. There are the ones that are too long and you end up putting it in one side and it comes out the other. Finally there are the ones that have some kind of a fancy notch in them that requires a special European tool to get the job done.

Even their barbecue display left me somewhat bewildered. I can get as excited as the next guy about having a great backyard barbecue, but some of the ones they had at this store wouldn't fit in the average backyard. Oh sure, there were the little ones that would hold a couple of burgers and maybe a small chicken. I swear one barbecue on display would hold a couple of head of cattle and a small ostrich. Looking at its price tag, I don't think I'd be able to afford meat for a couple of years after buying it. Its flame control dials had six settings, low, medium, high, towering inferno, global warming, and gates of hell.

I even found the parking lot to be a bit bewildering. One whole section was cordoned off to make room for an Elvis impersonator. I'm not sure what the connection is between hardware and an Elvis from his overweight, sequin-encrusted period. I was even a bit confused to discover that the parking spots reserved for disabled people were located as far from the entrances as possible.

My biggest confusion came when I was sitting in the car slowly moving through the clogged traffic trying to get out of the parking lot. I realized that, after spending nearly an hour wandering around a store as big as a good-sized cattle ranch; a store with several million products I don't know how to use; we had left without picking up the one thing we had gone in there to buy. To be honest, I couldn't even remember what it was.

Just to be on the safe side, I jiggled the handle on the toilet when I got home.

I Need No Fault Insurance For Stock Crashes

I spent the weekend with fifty or sixty investment brokers. One of them just happened to by my wife. They attended seminars, while I got to relax around the hotel and attend the much more important events - breakfasts, lunches, cocktail receptions, and dinner.

These poor folks are all living under the delusion that they can watch various indicators and determine what the markets will do. My wife has a bit of an advantage over the others, because she is constantly aware of the markets biggest indicator - me.

Oh, I don't pretend to be knowledgeable about the stock market, mutual funds, or government bonds. Quite the contrary; I know very little about them; just enough to make it look like I know what she's talking about when she tries to explain some stock to me during a hockey game. In fact, I have just about the right amount of investment understanding to get myself into financial trouble. That's why I'm such a good market indicator. If I think a company sounds like it might be worth investing in, everyone else should take that as an indicator that the company is about to go down the toilet.

I can read the financial pages of a newspaper as well as the next guy. I don't, but I could do it if I the right situation arose. That situation would probably only occur if someone pointed a gun at my head and forced me to read it. I've read some dull and boring articles in my life. I've even written some dull and boring articles. Nothing can quite compare to the stock market reports. "CRAP 52-1/2 51-1/4 54, CRUD 23-3/4 22 24-1/4" The only way I could hope to translate that into something remotely meaningful would be if my mother hadn't thrown out my Lone Ranger Secret Decoder Ring.

I understand that it's important to invest in a diversified portfolio. OK, no I don't, but it sounds like something I would say if I did know what it means.

I've invested in resource-based companies. I bought a natural gas company for $18.00 a share. The company apparently had all sorts of good things coming their way. Naturally the good things went by the boards and I ended up selling it at $6.00 a share. That was the indicator the market was looking for. As soon as I sold, the company's stock started to climb. It split three shares for one, and is now trading at around $40.00 a share.

Everybody and their brothers were investing in technology stocks in the late 1990's. When I finally got into that market sector, I bought into a well-known company at over $100.00 a share. My investment triggered panic in the stock markets, sending that stock cascading down a waterfall of sell orders. I think it's worth about $5.00 now; not the shares, the whole company.

The dot-com boom looked like it was going to make anyone who invested in an Internet start-up company a fortune. I managed to turn the boom into a bomb. The investment community should have seen the writing on the wall when someone was foolish enough to offer me stock options in their company in return for sitting on their advisory board. Obviously I wasn't invited to the board for my financial knowledge. The company was developing online services for writers and journalists. By the time I decided to find out what those options were worth the company's phones had been disconnected.

It's obvious that the stock market just isn't the right investment vehicle for me. Given the choice I can think of a lot of other investments I can understand a lot better. I could put my money into tangible investments like Wayne Gretzky hockey cards, die-cast cars from the 1950's, and the "Scandals Of The Royal Family" commemorative plate set.

I could, but you just know my wife would never go for it, don't you?

Diane thinks I should be putting my money into blue chip stocks. Apparently she isn't talking about the company that produces those colored tortilla chips. She thinks I should entrust her with my vast and varied investment portfolio. She'd have me liquidate all my hockey cards on E-Bay to free up some investment dollars for her to manage.

I don't think I'll do it. It's not that I don't trust her. I just don't think having a client with my luck would be all that good for her reputation in the business.

Still, if she was to handle my investments we could at least be assured of some return. She'd get a commission on my losing transactions.

Who Dumped All This White Crap On My Sidewalk?

The weather outside is frightful.

It's been over ten years since I wrote a column called, 'Disaster Strikes Vancouver, Many Left Without Access To Cappuccino" about the joys and thrills of having snow fall in Vancouver. Well, it's snowing again. Thousands of people are trying to start the day without benefit of Starbucks®. They'll be panicked by the storm, grouchy because they think they are the only ones who should be allowed to skid sideways down the hill on their street, and sleepy due to the missed caffeine hit.

Face it; we're not really true Canadians because we don't spend several months of each year shoveling our driveways. Snow is just not something we cope with very well on those rare occasions when it does collect on our roads and sidewalks. We've been inundated with white powder. I know that several of the cities where my columns appear have a severe white powder problem, but that's something people snort up their noses. If anyone tried to snort this white powder they'd get frostbite in their sinuses.

A few weeks ago we all watched with a sense of bemused indifference as Buffalo, New York was buried in snow. Frankly I think that's what you deserve if you live in Buffalo. If anything the snow hid a lot of the dirt and improved the overall appearance of the city. At the same time we were starting to see crocuses poking through the ground, and some of the cherry trees were starting to blossom. Spring had sprung around here, just as it always does in January.

Spring retreated yesterday. The snow started falling overnight and by morning we were faced with a full-scale winter storm. It continued for most of the day and through the next night. We are now dealing with really deep snow. In some parts of the city they've gotten as much as three inches of the stuff.

Call out the troops. Declare the city a disaster area. Airlift in a supply of food, snow tires and galoshes. We're in trouble here!

I grew up in Ontario so I know what a real snowstorm can do. The trouble is, I have lived on the West Coast for twenty-five years, and I can become just as easily panicked by a couple of millimeters of snow as the next Vancouverite.

It's especially hazardous for me to venture out in weather like this. When you are balanced on a couple of crutch tips on an icy sidewalk you really are taking your life into your own hands. Crutches seem to have a mind of their own when they get a bit of snow beneath them. The only thought they ever seem to have is to see how fast and how hard they can make me fall over. Even though I now have an assistance dog, her attitude seems to be that if I want to go out in the snow, I'm on my own.

Tragically there have been a few deaths attributed to this storm. Somehow I think if someone dies and gets to the Canadian section of heaven, they won't be let in if they admit they died in three inches of snow. There are probably signs eighteen inches up the gate that say, "It must be this deep before you can claim a snow related death as your reason for admission." If a Canadian dies in anything less they're probably sent to that one section of hell where it does actually freeze over.

Most Vancouver area residents have the same attitude toward snow removal. It's best summed up by the official motto of the city works yard, "Et'slay ustjay aitway untilyay ityay eltsmay."

The translation is, "Let's just wait until it melts."

As a result offices and schools are all but abandoned today.

Actually, looking out my office window, the snow is quite pretty, in a sort of Christmas card sort of way. If this had arrived on Christmas Eve I could almost have felt thankful for it. A white Christmas only happens a very few times each century out here. I miss it, but only about as much as I miss the feel of slush in my shoes.

According to the TV weatherman, we may see this snow stick around for a few days. That sounds like a recipe for cabin fever. I'll warn you right now. If next week's column is just a random collection of letters and numbers, you'll know the snow has sent me over to the dark side.

Somebody Call A Doctor

I Feel Like I'm Fixin' To Die

Plenty of people have said, from time to time, that I am a sick person. Now I really am a sick person. I'm feeling funny; something that normally makes it difficult to write funny.

And I have a column due today.

I spent last weekend in Washington, DC. The conference I was attending, BookExpo-America, had consumed close to 6,000 hotel rooms. A police conference took another huge number of suites. The Senate and Congress were in session so even more were in use by the politicians, lobbyists, and other hangers-on.

I ended up staying in a very old hotel a few blocks from the convention center, while my colleagues at my publishers ended up somewhere in Virginia. The hotel was OK. The room was clean. It had a fairly new bed, a good TV, and an internet connection, which are the top criteria I normally put on my list when looking for accommodation.

I guess I'm going to have to amend that list.

Apparently, hotel rooms with air conditioners that were installed sometime during the Johnson Administration can be a health risk. In this case, I think it might have been Andrew Johnson's Administration, not Lyndon's. Mold grows on the condensers. When they run, the mold can end up in the lungs of unsuspecting columnists trying to avoid a twenty-minute train trip to and from the convention center by staying in older, closer hotels.

In 1976, a group of American Legion members learned about this the hard way. On the upside, they got Legionnaire's Disease named after their organization.

By the third morning, I was feeling stuffed up and had a cough. I thought my old allergies were acting up. When I used to live in the eastern half of the continent, my hay fever would always move into overdrive at this time of year. It always seemed to coincide with final exams in school, which always provided me with a great excuse for the numbers on my report cards.

I didn't sleep the last two nights, because every time I nodded off, I would start to cough. By the time I got home, I felt like I was drowning.

My doctor has given me drugs and one of those inhaler things that sick kids in made for TV movies are always losing.

It's playing havoc with my plans and schedules. I've had to cancel part of my appearance tour for the coming weeks. In order to avoid disrupting my wife's sleep, I have been spending the nights on the living room sofa.

It's only fair, because when she is sick, I spend the nights on the living room sofa. Even through sickness, I manage to maintain my role as a freaking saint around here.

Pneumonia is not fun, and I'm not just talking about trying to spell it. Words like that always remind me about all those times when I would be the last kid picked for the team in grade-school spelling bees. But that's another painful story for another less painful time.

While it may not be fun, there are always a few hidden benefits to everything. For example, pneumonia appears to be great exercise.

After a prolonged coughing fit, all the muscles in my abdomen and chest - the ones I normally shelter under a protective layer of flab - feel like they've been through two weeks of Marine Corps boot camp.

It even works on some of the muscle groups that are often ignored by normal exercise regimens. Few people think about the muscles that hold their eyeballs in place. After coughing continuously for five or ten minutes, you'll be glad those muscles are there and doing their jobs. Each coughing fit strengthens them. By the time I recover, I should be able to out hit Barry Bonds by batting my eyelids.

I'm supposed to be getting lots of rest and drinking plenty of fluids. Fun fluids like beer, wine and whiskey aren't on the list. I think I should probably drink a bottle of that fluid they gave me before I had a colonoscopy.

It won't do anything for the pneumonia, but I'll be afraid to cough.

Recovering With Documentaries

Having pneumonia doesn't leave you with much energy to for anything except coughing, although as I am improving there does seem to be a bit of reserve available for hacking and wheezing.

I've now spent two weeks, not moving too far from the living room sofa. I've learned two things about myself during this period. I can sit through some pretty boring television shows, and I am not all that good at computer solitaire. According to the statistics on my solitaire game, the computer is ahead eighty-seven games to three.

Ever the optimist, I'm now calling it a best of one hundred and seventy five series.

Even with more than one hundred television channels coming in to my set, there aren't many shows I would normally watch. It all changes when you get sick. You know you have pretty much hit rock bottom when you can sit through a half-hour documentary on the 1919 Boston Molasses Explosion.

It's clear that much of the television programming during the day is not aimed at my gender. It isn't the content of the programming that leads me to that conclusion. It's the advertising. No matter how liberated I try to be, I cannot bring myself to have an interest in a product bearing the slogan, "Have a happy period."

In fact, like most men, when those ads come on, I am seriously tempted to put my hands over my ears and start singing, "Na-na-na! I can't hear you." I just haven't had the strength to do it this week.

On a similar vein, a documentary on the problems women face with menopause would never be high on my must-see-TV list. That said, when the other channels were showing reruns of M*A*S*H, fashion shows, home renovation competitions, and news about the latest terror threats, it seemed like the lesser of all evils.

It's always been very clear to me what causes almost all of the problems women face during menopause. It's not the hormonal changes they are going through. It's the fact that the men they are married to are not nearly sensitive enough to the hormonal changes they are going through.

TV shows never say that, but just ask any woman going through the experience and she will be more than happy to explain it to you.

At least the ones I know would.

Anytime.

Anywhere.

Of course, some daytime television brings back memories. I watched a show the other day featuring a pregnant woman. She called to her husband to put his hand on her stomach to feel the baby move.

I can remember those days. When Diane was pregnant for the first time, each flutter in her belly would leave me sitting beside her with my hand on her stomach waiting to feel something. I often had to wait a long time, especially, when the demand to feel the baby move came in the middle of the night when I thought I'd rather be sleeping.

It was especially long when she first felt the baby move and wanted to share the experience. By that point in the pregnancy, I had learned it was safest to just go along with whatever I was told to do, even if it meant losing the feeling from my elbow to my fingers waiting for a flicker of movement.

Watching that show made me think. That baby is now twenty-six, living in our spare room, and I am waiting for him to move again.

Falling asleep with the remote control in your hand can have some surprising results. The need to cough woke me from a brief nap the other afternoon. When I finally was able to stop coughing, I thought I had given myself a brain injury. It took a moment to realize I had not lost my ability to understand language; I just didn't understand the language coming through the TV. The channel had been switched to one delivering the news in Cantonese.

Since it was better than anything else that was on at that moment, I left it. It was almost as interesting as the half hour documentary on the 1919 Boston Molasses Explosion.

Reducing My Personal Colossalness

As we enter a new year, many people will be making the same old resolution that they have made each year for decades. This year, I am going to lose weight.

For most, it lasts until shortly after midnight on January first, when they pass the desert tray at the New Year's Eve party they are attending.

A few months ago, I discovered a great way to shed extra weight. I don't know if it works for women, but I am living proof that it does for husbands. I am about forty pounds lighter today than I was at the beginning of June. So what brought about this miracle?

My wife decided to lose weight.

Basically, when Momma ain't eatin' ice cream, ain't nobody eatin' ice cream.

She's eating healthy foods, watching her intake, and has eliminated all of those food groups that fall into the fun category. Even if we go out to eat, I am forced to consider the healthy alternative, because, should I decide to order a bacon double cheese burger I will get one of those withering looks wives can do so well.

I'm already withered enough, thank you very much.

Living with a spouse who is determined to shed extra poundage is a little like living with someone who has just quit smoking or drinking. You've all been around people like that. They are more than happy to tell you about all the reasons you should not partake in the product selections they would have willing joined you in consuming just a few weeks ago.

I haven't seen the inside of a donut in six months. I'm beginning to show signs of withdrawal. The three closest donut shops to my home have had to lay off staff. The Chamber of Commerce in Hershey, Pennsylvania may have needed an emergency meeting to determine how to deal with the impact on their town's economy, if I stopped eating chocolate.

They needn't worry. Whatever money is not going to fast food stores and candy shops is making its way into the economy through clothing stores. Diane has dropped five dress sizes. She is single handedly keeping two fashion stores and a tailor in business.

I put on quite a bit of weight after the accident that left me partially paralyzed in 1990. To put it in simple terms, I added the weight equivalent of an average eighth-grader to my bulk. This happened because my activity level took a nosedive, while my appetite for bacon double cheeseburgers stayed pretty much the same as it had always been.

My doctor has suggested I take up swimming to increase my activity; however, swimming to me is simply staying alive in the water when I can't touch the bottom. It's something I would do if I was ever thrown overboard from anything ranging in size from a canoe to a cruise liner.

As a result, I have stayed away from situations that called for me to be in a canoe or a cruise liner.

Some people seem to think my longstanding opposition to certain vegetables is the main reason for my weight. In actual fact, it is those vegetables that have helped me reduce my food consumption over the years. Just the smell of broccoli is enough to make me lose my appetite for all the other food that may be sharing space on the plate.

It's no secret, but that's why fast food chains have never introduced the broccoli double cheeseburger.

There was a bit of a concern about the impact of losing weight on my image. Over the years, I have developed a certain stage presence based on my admission that I am big for my age. Several people, who have seen me in recent weeks, have suggested that I limit how much weight I lose, so as not to adversely affect my image.

I think they have more confidence in my ability to shed pounds than I do. Even if I lost a lot more weight, I would still be big for my age. In fact, I am targeting just being big for my age, instead of enormous for my age.

I have a ways to go, but I am down to being vast for my age.

You Could Say I'm Unfeeling

Having a spinal cord injury definitely has its downside. In fact, I often fall on my downside, which is why I have Tara, my Labrador retriever assistance dog. She can help me back to my feet if and when my downside hit's the ground's upside.

It's now been sixteen years since I was involved in what I like to call my golfing accident. I was on my way to play golf when another driver thought it was more important to find the cassette tape he had dropped on the floor of his car, than to watch where he was going.

Unfortunately, I had stopped between him and where he was going.

I've often been told how lucky I am. I still have enough feeling below the waist to allow me to walk with crutches clipped to my arms. I have enough use of my right leg to drive a car, although because of the great loss of function on my left side, I am prohibited from driving a car with a standard transmission.

I think that's why my wife would like to buy a sports car with a standard transmission. She knows I couldn't drive it, and all the fun would be hers.

There is one rather large upside to losing much of the surface sensation on my legs. From time to time I will see a large bruise on my leg and think, "Gee, I bet that really hurts."

I learned a few weeks ago that not feeling an injury to my legs may not be the big advantage I thought it was.

It started out fairly innocuously. I didn't change the position of my legs enough during a four-hour drive. Anyone else would feel their legs starting to get uncomfortable after that length of time, and I am usually pretty good about remembering to move from time to time. For some reason on this occasion, I forgot.

As I drove, my leg rubbed on a rough patch on the inside of my boot. Two blisters developed on my calf. I didn't know they were there, until I noticed them later that night, once again thinking, "Gee, I bet those hurt."

I didn't think of them again until four days later. As I was getting ready for bed at about one o'clock in the morning, I noticed my leg was bright red from the knee to the ankle. Clearly, I had developed a rather severe infection, but still did not feel it. One look told me it was a fairly serious infection, so I decided to drive myself to the emergency ward to have it checked out.

I spent the next several days visiting the hospital twice a day for an intravenous injection of antibiotics. I had to walk around with the IV connection taped to my wrist. At a party an American friend of mine asked what it was.

"Well," I whispered to him, "because I've eaten a lot of pancakes over the years, and there is currently a maple syrup shortage in my country, I'm part of a top-secret Canadian syrup reclamation program. They've tapped me like a maple tree."

For a moment I thought he was going to buy it, but then he remembered who he was talking to. It's hard to pull the wool over someone's eyes, no matter how gullible they might be, when you have a reputation for being a professional smart-ass.

It probably serves me right that the next day I noticed a rash developing in places that I can feel. (Yes. There too.) My body decided that it didn't really like all of those antibiotics that were being pumped into me. It retaliated by making me allergic to them. I am already allergic to two other types of antibiotics. I'm starting to run out of options.

In order to combat the allergic reaction the doctor put me on steroids and antihistamines, both of which would make me fail a urine test at the Olympics. I guess it will give me another reason that I'll have to rule out competing in the 2010 Winter Games.

And now I'll never get elected to the Baseball Hall of Fame.

Remembering My Pasture As I Head To The Future

My Wife Can Beat The Forces of 'Evel'

I haven't visited Idaho for a few years. The last time I was there, it proved that it is a strange little state full of dusty fields and pastures, and reminded me of a painful moment in my own personal pasture.

You can drive for hours along I-84 and not see another living soul. Even when you do see the hand of man on this stark landscape, it seems to have a certain weirdness to it.

Take Idaho Falls. About 20 years after the town was established, someone decided that it might be a good idea if it had a real, honest to goodness waterfall to go with its name. So, sometime around the 1900, they built one. Prior to that, the Snake River ran over a few rocks that created a bit of white water but certainly nothing resembling a waterfall.

You might remember the Snake River. Back in the 1974, Evel Kneivel decided to try to fly his motorcycle across the Snake River Canyon. It sounds like a pretty exciting way to spend an otherwise boring afternoon in Idaho - at least it would be if he had successfully flown his motorcycle across the Snake River Canyon. Unfortunately for Mr. Kneivel, he will never know, because he failed.

Spectacularly.

I was reminded of that event when I pulled into Twin Falls in the fall of 1999 for an appearance at a local bookstore. There were no signs welcoming me to Twin Falls, but there were hundreds welcoming back Evel Kneivel for the 25th anniversary celebration of his spectacular failure.

When I look back at my life, and at the things I have attempted that didn't go quite the way I planned, I can say with absolute surety, I hope no one remembers what they were 25 years after they occurred. Even if they do remember, I hope they don't plan on inviting me back to relive the moment.

I have on occasion referred to my wife, as Diane Kneivel, or Evel Knirkland. She once launched a Honda Civic, and remained aloft for roughly the same amount of time as Evel Kneivel did over the Snake River Canyon.

OK, so it's not a long time in the air, but still, it's the effort people remember.

That event leaps back into my mind whenever I see movies or television shows involving car chases that include drivers launching surface to air Ford Mustangs, intercontinental ballistic Chevrolet Camaros, and nuclear Dodge Chargers. It occurred just a couple years after Evel's crash landing at the bottom of the canyon. It was probably Diane's most successful flight, if you judge success the same way certain budget airlines do. She managed to take-off, but nearly lost her passenger on landing. Unfortunately, her passenger was me.

I was convinced I was going to die.

When we landed I felt like I was going to die.

Within seconds of landing, I wanted to die.

On any other day, I might have settled for just being terrified, but on this particular day, Diane was driving me home from the hospital after major liver surgery. I already felt rotten. I just wanted to get home to my own bed after several weeks in a hospital whose nursing staff behaved as if their previous jobs were in Jonestown dispensing Kool-Aid.

I sat in the passenger seat, with my head propped on a pillow against the side window. My eyes were closed, and Diane did most of the talking. I didn't really feel capable of sustained intelligent conversation when every pebble she hit made it feel like the stitches in my abdomen were going to rip out. I also wasn't thinking about the route Diane was taking, or that one particular culvert along the way that the frost had lifted creating a perfect Honda launch ramp.

Diane wasn't thinking about that culvert either.

As soon as we hit it, the whole world grew quite around us. Diane stopped talking about how glad she was to finally get me home again. There was no longer any noise from the tires on the road. I stopped breathing entirely. The flight seemed to last longer than the Wright Brothers initial attempt. It was a smooth flight. It was not such a smooth landing. The second and third bounces weren't all that smooth either.

Nor were they quiet. The shock absorbers banged. The tires squealed. I screamed. Diane screamed. With all that noise, I'm sure every dog within a five mile radius decided it better start barking.

I think we may have even stampeded a herd of cows or two.

Evel Knievel may have gotten all the publicity for his jump, but I'd be willing to bet that my wife in a Honda Civic can get further across the Snake River Canyon than he and his Skycycle any day.

I Was A Different Sort Of Bagboy

I was asked the other day about my first job, not counting a paper route when I was twelve. I'm sure the people doing the survey were expecting me to talk about any one of the stereotypical first jobs so many people have. I don't think they were prepared for mine.

I'm not sure if you are.

I did not enter the working world manning the grill at a fast food restaurant. I didn't wait on tables or stock shelves in a grocery store. Those are normal jobs for normal people.

And we all know how normal I am, don't we?

My first job was about as far removed from normal as possible. I filled large bags with air.

It was a summer job, tucked in between grade eleven and grade twelve. I became proficient in attaching a hand pump to a nozzle, and filling the bag to capacity with air; just the sort of thing that utilized, without overtaxing, my technical abilities.

These were not small bags. They were roughly the size of the garbage bags used for disposing garden waste. They held a lot of air.

Four times a day, I would visit five locations in the city of London, Ontario, stand on a street corner, and fill my oversized bright blue plastic bag with air by squeezing the hand pump several hundred times. The bags were then returned to a laboratory at the University of Western Ontario, where the chemical contents of the air could be analyzed for pollutants.

That job involved passing the air through a fluid inside a machine that was clearly marked, "Gordon Kirkland is not allowed to touch this machine."

Apparently, there was some concern about combining my technical abilities with an infrared spectrometer that cost several thousand times my weekly salary.

I collected my samples at a quiet university campus location, a busy downtown intersection, across the street from a large brewery, in the middle of an industrial area, and in a predominantly residential area. Over the course of the summer, I visited those sites at some point during every one of the twenty-four hours of each of the seven days of the week. That is eight hundred and forty bags of air.

OK. So it didn't give me much in the way of intellectual stimulation, but it had its moments.

One night, at about two o'clock in the morning, I stood quietly filling my bag with air at the busy downtown intersection. The streets were empty except for the occasional cop, and a wino or two.

I was alone for the first half of the chore, but eventually a lone figure staggered down the street. At first, I thought he might have been a city employee checking the sturdiness of the light posts, because he grabbed each one he came to and hung on for a moment or two.

By the time he was a couple of light posts away, I could tell he was more than slightly inebriated. A lit match within ten feet of him could have blown us both into the middle of the next week.

He stood, clinging to the closest light post, and stared at me.

"Whatcherthinkyerdoin?" he managed to say, stringing all of his words into one.

"I'm checking the atmosphere here," I said.

"Whatcherwannadothatfor?" he countered.

"To see if the air on this planet is safe for my fellow Zenukobian warriors before we attack and colonize it." I said, proving I could be just as much of a smartass at sixteen as I am at fifty-three.

His eyes widened and his chin dropped. He turned on his heels and quickly retraced his steps down the street, once again testing every light post along the way. He may have warned them to get out of town before the attack.

I've often wondered if it was a sobering experience for him, or if he is still sitting on a street corner wearing an aluminum foil cap to protect him from the Zenukobians.

I can't say I have ever needed to draw on the knowledge I gained filling large bags with air, but as first jobs go, though, it was certainly more memorable than flipping burgers.

I Just Don't See Eye-To-Eye With Goats

I don't like goats and goats don't like me.

It wouldn't bother me in the least if someone decided to take every last one of them to a slaughterhouse. While the extinction of a species might be a sad thing, in the case of goats, it should be a cause for celebration.

I think I have a fairly solid reason for my feelings towards the species. It is also true that goats do not like me, and this statement has been proven beyond any reasonable doubt.

During the seventies, a time my wife and I now refer to as those days when we didn't need two or three lenses in our glasses, we owned a small hobby farm in Ontario. Bruce and Lo, friends of ours down the road and a couple not normally predisposed to being stupid, bought a couple of goats. That's how I came to discover I do not like goats and they do not like me.

Frankly, goats are just weird. If you've ever looked a goat in the eye, you'll see right away that something went terribly wrong during the evolution of this creature. Its pupils are not round. Goat eyes are centered by black rectangles. I may be prejudiced toward round-pupiled animals like dogs and horses, but rectangular pupils are just wrong, wrong, wrong.

There was a wild plant that grew in the area. Unlike the cultivated version that brings in a fortune to people who grow it in the basements of rented houses, wild cannabis is a fairly small plant that grows along fences, ditches, and railroad tracks in that area.

Goats loved the stuff.

The average goat's intellect is not something that would put it on a cognitive par with anything smarter than a small bolder or a rotted out tree stump. A stoned goat's intellect is even lower. They would eat the stuff, and then spend the rest of the day staring out into the fields, rocking slightly from side to side, with a bemused sort of "Oh Wow! Look at... uhh... what is there to eat?" look on their already stunned faces.

Giving an animal whose sole purpose in life is to eat 24/7 the munchies is just asking for trouble.

There may be some people who came out of the sixties, like a certain president who didn't inhale, who aren't aware that when someone ingests the active ingredient found in cannabis, their pupils enlarge. It might not look that odd in humans, dogs, or horses, but, as I've told you, a goat has rectangular pupils. Coming eye-to-eye with a stoned goat was just not something you'd ever forget.

You might be thinking it's pretty shallow to develop a prejudice against an entire species based solely on eye shape. You'd probably be right. I have another bit of evidence against these creatures I believe gives me the right to dislike them, and proves they dislike me.

We were asked to take care of the animals on Bruce and Lo's farm one weekend. I had no problem feeding the horses, cleaning their stalls, or getting them out into the pasture in the morning and back into the barn at night. In fact, being a horse enthusiast, I quite enjoyed it.

One evening, both Diane and I were tired. We took care of the duties in the barn, and started to head back to our car. Bruce had installed an intricate chain and lock combination on the paddock gate. We decided to skip dealing with it and just crawl under the gate. I held the chain up for Diane, and then I bent over to crawl under it.

That's when my dislike for goats jelled into a deep-seated hatred.

It must have looked like something from a cartoon. I made a perfect 3-point landing beside my wife in the lane. Unfortunately the three points that skidded into the gravel were both palms and my face. One of the useless, reefer-mad, square-pupiled goats butted me squarely in the butt, thereby hastening my departure from the paddock.

I'm not sure what hurt more, my palms, my face, my butt, or my feelings. It was probably the latter because my dear wife showed her sincere sympathy for my predicament by laughing hysterically.

So there you have it. Some of you goat-lovers out there might not like it, but I will say it until my dying day. I don't like goats, and they don't like me. Round them up and send them to a slaughterhouse.

...and if you need help, just give me a call.

Turtle Takes Taste Of Teutonic Teen

I get some odd stories crossing my desk, and from time to time they bring back memories. One that hit this week fit that bill, and caused me to wince at the same time. Just the headline alone was enough to make me consider putting on protective gear before reading the rest of the story.

"Snapping Turtle Bites Boy's Penis"

Apparently, someone released a North American snapping turtle into a lake in Germany. The turtle bit a fifteen-year-old boy through his swimsuit, and again on his hand as he scrambled to get away from it.

When I was young we had a summer cottage on a lake about one-hundred miles north of Toronto. It had a resident population of snapping turtles.

On one occasion, long before I came to be, my father was clearing rocks from the lake bottom to make way for a new wharf in a protected bay behind the cottage. He had a great deal of difficulty pulling one rock from the bottom, but eventually managed to dislodge it.

As he told the story, had that "rock" been facing the opposite direction, I never would have been born. He would have suffered the same fate as the German boy, coming face-to-place with a snapping turtle.

It wasn't uncommon to find snapping turtles sunning themselves on the rocks around our cottage. We'd also see them swimming along with their heads out of the water. They had a face that only a mother snapping turtle could love.

After one late evening fishing trip, I left a string of five or six smallmouth bass tied to the wharf, with plans to clean them for breakfast the next morning. When I went to get them, I discovered that I had provided a buffet banquet for a turtle. He left me with a couple of heads, but little else.

We were taught to give the snapping turtles as much room as they wanted. My mother always knew she could get us out of the water by simply saying, "Oh... Is that a snapping turtle coming around the point?" No one wanted to be in the water anywhere near a turtle.

When Diane and I started going to the cottage after we were married, we'd take our border collie along with us. He loved to swim, and would dive off the wharf after tennis balls all day long if you'd let him, and if your throwing arm lasted.

On one memorable occasion, Diane and my father were sitting on the wharf with the dog. Dad would throw the ball as high as he could over the lake so it would make a large splash when it hit the water, making it easier for the dog to spot.

It may have been similar to what he did with that turtle he pulled from the lake bottom years earlier.

I was snorkeling nearby, and had moved underwater to the area in front of the wharf. Just as I surfaced, the tennis ball descended. The back of my head and the front of the ball collided, nearly rendering me senseless. I was convinced I had surfaced underneath a snapping turtle. I did what every other red-blooded man would do in that situation.

I flailed my arms wildly and screamed like a little girl.

You really shouldn't scream with a snorkel in your mouth, especially, if the top of is still under water. It just gives you one more thing to worry about. On top of being convinced a snapping turtle is about to show you how it got its name, you are also painfully aware you have just filled your lungs with lake water and are about to drown. Having my wife and father a few feet away on the wharf did me absolutely no good.

People who are laughing hysterically make lousy lifeguards.

Snapping turtles were put on the International Endangered Species list just last month. The turtle is now protected, even so far from its natural home. As for the bitten boy, I am sure he will make sure he is also protected the next time he goes into that lake.

I know I would.

Forget The Highway, I Can Get Lost On The Information Side Street

The Problem Is Somewhere Between My Keyboard And The Back Of My Chair

I replaced my computer last week. For most people, that's not a particularly difficult thing to do. For those of us who can get lost on the information dirt road, it can be a heart wrenching process.

When you start over with a new computer it can be like starting over with a new wife - not that I have any personal experience with that, but based on what friends and family have told me, it might be easier to get used to a new spouse than a new computer.

Over time, you get your computer to do things the way you want them done. You come to expect the screen to look the way you want it to, and you want to be able to get to the programs you need without any great difficulty.

Starting off afresh is like looking at a blank slate. Nothing you want or need is there, or if it is, it isn't where you expect it to be. I have a lot of programs I use every day to get my work done. None of them were present on the new computer when I turned it on.

Those who understand these things don't seem to understand that those of us without too much of a clue about computers will find this sudden disappearance of the programs we know, love, and depend upon just a little bit off-putting

Right now, my put is so far off I can barely find it.

Those same people who understand computers will tell you it is a simple process of installing the programs you want on the new computer. Just take the computer discs for the programs and put them into the computer. It will do most of the rest.

The discs... those are those round shiny silver things, right?

I was supposed to put them someplace where I would remember them. I just forgot where that was after I put them there.

You need to understand what my office looks like. I have stacks of papers and books scattered throughout the room. I could probably jumpstart a community recycling program with all the paper that I have sitting around here. I have file cabinets full to overflowing and bookcases that would burst if I tried to add another book to them. My desk groans whenever I add another piece of paper to one of the piles.

And amidst all of that, you think I might be able to easily find a computer disc I last used sometime in 2003?

I don't think so.

After a lot of searching I managed to lay my hands on most of the discs but was immediately faced with another problem. Apparently, in amongst all of the paperwork that came with the discs in the first place was some sort of code that I was supposed to keep in order to reinstall the software at a later date.

These codes are nothing like the ones that you see spies using on old war movies. You cannot simply type a phrase like "The pig will sing under the full moon if the duck is dancing on the roof of the castle," and expect to gain access to you programs.

These codes look something like "AA4G-W8R5-TBUL-559D-Q77L-MM99-MIC-KEY-MOU-SE."

Who could remember that for more than a nanosecond or two?

Computer software companies say this access code is there to stop people from stealing the software. I remain convinced there is another ulterior motive for them to include a code the CIA would have trouble deciphering. Without it, people like me will have to go out and buy new copies of their software if they replace their computers. Planned customer forgetfulness probably adds more to their corporate financial statements than planned product obsolescence.

Of course there is always the possibility I will learn a valuable lesson from this experience. I could get myself organized and keep a record of all of those codes and where I have stored the discs so the next time this happens I will not have these problems again.

Yea, right; even I'm not naive enough to think that's ever going to happen.

GPS: The Global Pestering System

There are four things you should know about my wife. They all seem to be unrelated, but they come together from time to time. That can be scary.

First, she is a brilliant woman. She even understands complicated math, something that has eluded me since the fifth grade, which is very helpful in her role as a very successful stock broker.

Secondly, and not quite as complimentary, she has the directional capabilities of an intoxicated fruit fly.

Despite this, she still wants to control the car, even when she is in the passenger seat. I regularly find myself double checking to make sure those are actually my hands on the steering wheel.

Finally, She is one of the most difficult women on the planet to get to give you gift ideas.

Those four characteristics have all come to the forefront over the holiday season.

Early last year I wrote about my wife's somewhat deficient sense of direction. While the woman is extremely smart in so many ways, trying to get her to go from Point A to Point B can be an exercise in futility.

Before we met, Diane had risen to the highest level of the Girl Guides organization. One would think that in order to do that, she would have to have some understanding of north and south. I've learned it is best to avoid giving her directions that include telling her to turn north or south, unless I expect her to end up one hundred miles east or west of her destination.

Frankly, I can't imagine how she survived those camping and hiking trips with the Girl Guides. I can only assume they didn't let her lead the way.

Diane will regularly tell me she thinks I should be in a different lane, or taking a different route. She remains convinced, despite her intoxicated gnat-like directional abilities, that I need her advice when I am behind the wheel.

It often makes me think about my father. He had a small sign installed in his car for my great aunt's benefit. It advised those who would like to comment on the driver's actions or choices of routes to take note of the mistletoe pinned to his coattails.

A few weeks ago, as the holiday season approached, I asked Diane what she would like for Christmas. Diane's childhood Christmases involved gifts of socks, underwear, and if she had been very, very good, she might get a new pair of pajamas. Even though we've been married for over thirty years, it's still hard to get her to think about asking for something.

When I posed the question, I assumed I would once again get the, "Oh, I don't know" answer. The speed and intensity of her answer surprised me.

"I'd like one of those things for the car that tells me how to get where I need to go," she said.

So began my research into global positioning systems, something we could have had factory installed in the new car we picked up less than a month before. They seem to range from something you would need a magnifying glass to try to see what is on the screen to large screens that double as DVD players, and I think they might also make toast and coffee, but I'm not sure about that.

I finally settled on one that has an ample screen and an internal voice that tells you when your turn is coming. Most importantly, for Diane's sake, it uses terms like left and right instead of north and south. It can readjust if you make a mistake and take a wrong turn, getting you back on the right track by the quickest possible route. It even keeps you posted on the distance left to your destination and estimates a time of arrival.

The instructions say it doesn't work well in Hawaii, but then I'm not sure how one would drive to Hawaii in the first place.

We installed it on the weekend. Almost immediately, I knew I was in trouble.

As I turned onto the street, the voice in the device told me to change lanes. Diane just smiled.

Just What I Need - A Computer With Nag Version 3.1

Technology is starting to get way ahead of me. To hear my sons speak, technology got ahead of me somewhere around the time that the wheel was invented. I might dispute that, but I have to admit they aren't that far off the mark.

Every morning I turn on my computer and I expect it to perform certain functions. I don't ask it how it does it. I don't care how it does it. I just want it to do what I want without any backtalk.

I had the ridiculous idea that the computer was the one thing I could control around here. After years of marriage, I know there is absolutely no way I am ever going to have the slightest bit of control over my wife. The last time I controlled anything about the lives of either of my sons was during the brief interval between birth and them learning to say, "Dad, I need a..."

When she was alive, I couldn't even control the dumbest dog to ever get lost on a single flight of stairs. What did that say for me? She's was about 93 in dog years. We went for walks on her schedule, not mine. She vocalized her contempt for just about everything. If she felt she wasn't getting a big enough share of whatever I was eating, she growled. If someone disturbed her sleep she made a sound that left no doubt about its translation from dog to English.

Worse still, she decided that the portion of the couch I preferred to watch TV from was hers. Whenever I walked into the living room, she'd open one eye and give me a look that could only mean, "Don't even think about asking me to move." If I forced her down she had her own way of retaliating that quickly returned control of the coveted spot on the couch. Her digestive tract aged along with the rest of her. She used that to her advantage by making the immediate vicinity uninhabitable to everyone but her.

Even the cat fled the room.

Now that I have a Labrador retriever, a dog smarter than the honor students people brag about on their bumper stickers, she controls my day by regularly pointing out that she needs me to open the dog biscuit box.

At least I'm good for something around here.

With so little control of my day-to-day life, is it any wonder that I am more than a bit concerned about the advances in computer technology. My computer now has a nag factor built into it. I thought owning a computer would let me tell it what to do. I guess, after the experience I've had with the kids and the dog, I should have known better. Every couple of days it tells me to upgrade its virus protection. It tells me when I have mail that needs to be read. It even tells me when the printer needs toner. I thought I'd finished following those kinds of demands when the kids were old enough to get up and get their own glass of water.

If all that isn't bad enough, I watched a report on the news this morning about computers that will send your car messages telling you where to go. Apparently the computer is going to communicate with all of the appliances in the house as well. That way it can act as their spokesperson. It will tell you when you need to buy milk, clean the oven, or throw out whatever is in that leftover container that has been there so long it's developed its own life form. Even worse, it will phone you and tell you the lawn needs watering.

Of course all of this development is made with the intent of making our lives easier. The computer will take care of chores the nontechnical among us find bewildering. I can't wait for the day when my computer can figure out the instructions for my DVD player.

Apparently some people want their computers to take on even more personal aspects of their lives. In Dubai, you can now divorce your wife simply by letting your computer send her three messages containing the phrase, "I divorce thee." That disturbs me. I'm not worried that my wife might decide to have her computer send me those three messages. I don't even care what that might mean for the economic situation of lawyers everywhere. I'm just afraid one morning I'll turn on the computer and it will have sent me a note divorcing me in order to run off with the microwave.

I'd really miss that microwave.

Like Father, Like Grandson

I was thinking the other day that my father would have been quite proud of my oldest son. Mike is in his final semester at college. I got bored with school before I could attain that educational milestone, but that's not especially what would have made Dad proud. Mike is majoring in something technical that I do not understand.

My father was a big fan of technical things I don't understand.

The computers Mike uses are the sort of thing you might have read about in science fiction novels when my father was alive. They might have even made it into magazines like Popular Mechanics and Popular Science, which regularly made predictions about what life would be like in the Twenty-first Century.

I don't know about you, but I don't have a car that converts to an airplane in my garage. We don't travel on highways imbedded with magnets that propel our vehicles without the need for steering wheels or accelerators. Somehow, those computers would seem just as futuristic to my father as anything those magazines. Still, if he could see his grandson at work on a computer, he'd be quite proud.

I guess certain skills must skip a generation. I have often mentioned my handyman skills, or rather my lack thereof. The fact that I didn't know the difference between a lathe and a router was always a bit disappointing to Dad, but he and Mike would have had a lot in common. My father was always interested in new things, and in figuring out how they worked. Dad built his own radios. Mike builds his own computers. Mike has taken apart various appliances and other electrical devices ever since he was about 10 -- sometimes with less than stellar results. Dad would take things apart to see if he could figure out how they worked and if he could improve them. He was like a precursor to Tim Allen's character on Home Improvement, complete with lots of grunting.

I can recall quite vividly one of Dad's more spectacular improvements. We had a kitchen drawer that was difficult to pull open. Nothing seemed to help get it to slide smoothly on its tracks. It took an almighty tug to get it to budge. We had all gotten quite used to that drawer. Still, it was a source of great consternation to my father. Things like that were supposed to work the way you expected them to, and he wouldn't be happy until that drawer did.

Dad worked for a company that developed a silicon solution that could be sprayed from an aerosol can. He knew just where to test the stuff. If silicon could make that kitchen drawer move smoothly, who knows what wondrous things it could be used for. He brought a sample home from work and applied it liberally to the sides, bottom and tracks of the flawed drawer. It was a miracle. The drawer slid in and out with ease. He was justifiably proud of his accomplishment, and waited with anticipation for my mother to discover the great improvement he had wrought. He was sure she'd be overjoyed.

Perhaps, looking at the event with the 20-20 vision hindsight offers, he just might have been advised to warn her.

If I close my eyes I can still picture the pandemonium that erupted a few minutes after Dad finished. He and I were sitting in the living room, when out in the kitchen there arose such a clatter. It didn't take too long to see what was the matter. My mother exited the kitchen running backwards with the offending drawer held high over her head like the Statue of Liberty and her torch. A collection of cooking utensils spread out in her wake from the place where she had given the drawer its usual tremendous tug to her eventual landing site in the front hall near the door.

I have to wonder just how closely Mike will follow in his grandfather's footsteps. Perhaps someday he will solve household problems with artificial intelligence. It isn't too difficult to picture him developing an artificially intelligent robot to take care of all the mundane kitchen duties he has never been very good about doing on his own anyway. I just hope that if he decides to lubricate a kitchen drawer he warns the robot. It might not be as forgiving as my mother was, especially if Mike laughs as hard as my father did that day.

It Must Be True. It Was In The News

Three Infidels Walk Into A Bar...

Like most authors, I am constantly on the lookout for ways to get my books to sell better. Over the years that's led to a great deal of travel, countless radio and TV appearances, and staying in touch with a lot of book reviewers.

Perhaps, I haven't been talking to the right ones.

Author Richard Blum seems to have run across the mother of all book reviewers. His book, *The Rogue State*, was ranked somewhere in the area of 209,000 in sales on Amazon until last week. One book review vaulted it into the top 30. It's any author's dream to get that kind of a response to a review.

In a tape released on January 19, 2006, Osama Bin Laden said he and his band of merry men were preparing more attacks in the United States. He advised his American viewers that, "It is useful for you to read the book 'The Rogue State.'"

I guess Blum's book is the first selection on the Osama Book Club.

I suppose, when you are camped out in the mountains of Afghanistan or Pakistan you have a lot of time on your hands. Reading is one of the few ways to pass the time. Somehow, I can't quite picture Osama and his boys sitting around a campfire singing show tunes and roasting marshmallows.

The whole Brokeback Mountain image doesn't quite fit either.

"I just don't know how to quit you, Osama"

See what I mean.

But a book club might just be the ticket for those long nights in the cave.

I've spoken to a number of book clubs over the years. The concept is that everyone present will have read the book of the week or month, and a lively discussion will ensue. Of course, there will always be a considerable amount of time spent eating finger sandwiches and socializing before the evening's discussion begins.

Again, I'm not sure how that part might work in an al-Qaeda book club.

"That's a lovely hooded thobe you're wearing tonight, Osama."

"Why, this old thing? I made it myself years ago."

Nope. It just doesn't sound like the kind of conversation you'd expect from the most wanted man on the planet.

Still, I have to take note of the incredible and rapid climb Blum's book took after the bin Laden endorsement. He may not be as powerful as Oprah, but he sure can get results for an author.

Now, if I can only figure out how I can get him to review one of my books.

I have a new book coming out at the end of March. *I Think I'm Having One Of Those Decades* will be my fourth book, and my third in the last three years. That's meant a lot of work has gone into the promotions, but I still have never had a positive nod from Osama.

I suppose part of the problem is that Osama likes to read books that are critical of American foreign policy. I'm just not that interested in writing about American foreign policy. Surely, Osama must like to come home from a long day of making videotapes for Al Jazeera, slip into something more comfortable, and read a good book, just for the relaxing pleasure of reading.

He may have even ordered a few volumes from the Book of the Month Club mistakenly thinking the titles were about something more in line with his philosophy. Perhaps he bought *The Bridges of Madison County*, hoping it was actually an engineering manual on the structural integrity of the bridges in Madison County. Who knows? He may even have a copy of *The Da Vinci Code* kicking around on a bookshelf in his cave. I'm sure he was disappointed when he found out it wasn't about deciphering secret messages between CIA operatives in Italy.

In that vein, you'd think he would have had his interest piqued by my second book, *Never Stand Behind A Loaded Horse*, thinking it was about the proper way to detonate a suicide Clydesdale.

Perhaps, if I really want Osama to boost my book sales with an endorsement, I should start writing stories with titles like, 'Three infidels walk into a bar...'"

News From The Relationship Front Lines

Hot, steamy, unbridled sex.

Now that I have your attention, I'd like to update you on the current information available about a subject that generally baffles most men. Relationships.

As you all know, my wife and I have been married for over thirty years. Sure, I married up, and by the time she discovered that, she was too tired to even think about wanting to train a new husband.

A study recently came to light, that says I have been doing something right all along.

I know. It surprised the heck out of me, too.

Apparently, 63 percent of the men and 73 percent of the women in the US and Canada believe a sense of humor is the most important trait in a perspective mate.

Physical attraction was the most important trait identified by men in France, Brazil, Greece, Japan and Britain. Mind you, the British may have misunderstood the question and thought the surveyors were asking about horses, if the future Queen Seabiscuit is any example of what the well dressed British aristocrat is looking for in a woman.

Forty percent of Portuguese men said they would look for intelligence over appearance. Is it any surprise that of the Australian men surveyed, a grand total of exactly zero percent of the male respondents selected intelligence.

All of that might be explained by the fact that British and Australian men admitted they often drank too much when trying to impress the opposite sex. German and Italian men take an entirely different approach – they lie about their finances. That may explain why seventy percent of German women admitted to lying about their marital status.

The study was conducted by that venerable old Canadian publisher of fine literature, Harlequin Enterprises. The results raise some questions about Harlequin's future book marketing plans in sixteen countries surveyed. For example:

- Will Canadian and American copies of *My Bodice Spontaneously Erupted* feature two lovers wrapped in each other's arms, laughing hysterically?
- Will the French and Italian versions show a muscular man leaning on the Porsche or Lamborghini that was conveniently parked beside his rusted out 1969 Ford Maverick?
- Will the Brazilian and Mexican versions, where eighty percent of the men admit to lying about their marital status, depict dark Latin men quickly trying to remove their wedding rings as the heroine approaches?

Of course, the British version will have a homely looking man with big ears, wearing a crown and looking lovingly into the deep reflective pools that are the eyes of his polo pony.

Of course, it will probably come as no surprise the survey found men the world over looked for beauty over brains when first meeting a woman. Even in those first meetings, the majority of women looked for a good sense of humor.

Oh, yes, yes, yes!

I'm sure you're all wondering, how all this translates into the animal kingdom. Another study found some interesting related data in bats. Why anyone is interested in the mating preferences and activities of bats is beyond me. Even so, the results were enlightening.

Syracuse University biologist Scott Pitnick led a research team of bat sex voyeurs who found that, in bat species where the females are promiscuous, the males with the largest... well... the... umm... OK, we're not talking about fingers and toes here...

Putting it into a sports analogy, let's just say the boy bats with the biggest bats and balls had the smallest brains. I have to wonder if it affects their ability to fly. Then again, maybe they don't need to fly.

While the study didn't mention if those species lived in Britain or Australia, I wonder if they also admitted to drinking too much when trying to meet a promiscuous girl bat.

On the other side of that coin, in the species where the females were faithful to their partners the males were smaller in the bat tingly places, and had larger brains.

So guys, the next time a woman tells you you have the brains of a bat, be sure to laugh a lot, and say, "Yeah, but we all know what that means, don't we?"

Animals Are A Danger To Man And Upholstery

Apparently, animals are causing a huge number of traffic accidents each year. You could say the accident that broke my spine was caused by a lower form of animal. He was looking for a cassette tape on the floor of his car when he drove into mine.

I've often thought of animal comparisons for that individual, and I have on several occasions referred to him as being at least part animal - that being the colorectal region of a horse.

We all know that suicidal raccoons, groundhogs and possums use the roads to end their lives. Obviously, these animals are not taking into account the potential danger they are presenting to humans and their upholstery when they venture out into traffic.

Deer are the biggest problem. Car/deer collisions killed 200 people in the United States alone in 2000, the last year for which statistics are available. They also resulted in over $1.5-billlion in damages.

A British driver recently reported the accident he was involved in was caused by a frozen squirrel that dropped from a tree and crashed through his windshield.

Rocky, the flying squirrel-cicle.

It isn't just wild animals. The domesticated ones are getting into the act, too. For example, over ninety people are killed each year in Namibia in traffic accidents caused by donkeys' preference for sleeping on warm paved roads. Thankfully, that isn't a problem here in North America. We already have enough jackasses on our roads – including the one who hit me.

I witnessed one severe accident involving an animal crashing through a driver's windshield. It wasn't a pretty sight. It was an even worse smell.

Several years ago, a driver ahead of me hit a skunk. The skunk was sent rocketing skyward by the car's rear tires. Thankfully, I was driving a Triumph TR7 at the time, and my low profile enabled the skunk to sail unobstructed above me.

The driver of the car behind me wasn't quite so lucky.

The skunk hit the man's windshield and landed on the passenger seat beside him. I don't know if there was still a little bit of terrified life left in the animal, or if it was just a post-mortem muscle spasm, but the skunk released the full contents of its scent emitting organ at that precise moment.

I think the driver may have released something else. Either way, he needed major corrective surgery to his clothes and upholstery, to say nothing of his sinuses.

My father always claimed he was nearly killed in a collision with a grasshopper. He was driving along, minding his own business, when a grasshopper leapt through his open side window. It struck his wire-rimmed glasses right at the bridge of his nose, causing them to be yanked from his ears and bent them a full one hundred and eighty degrees. He may have had an upholstery incident as well, but he never admitted to it.

The closest I have ever been to actually hitting an animal occurred over thirty years ago. My brother was at the wheel on a night enveloped in a thick fog.

It was foggy outside our heads too.

Suddenly, a pure white horse leapt across the road in front of us disappearing into the fog as fast as it had appeared. Neither of us said a word.

Finally, after a mile or two, my brother asked, "Did you see that?"

"What did you see?" I asked, not willing to mention the horse until he came out and said he had seen it too.

"Oh, nothing I guess," Jim said, equally unwilling to admit to seeing white horses appear and disappear.

"Did your nothing have a white tail and mane?" I asked.

"Maybe," he said. "Did yours?"

When it became clear we had both seen a white horse jump out of the fog (that's the fog outside our heads) and disappear back into it, we decided no one would believe us if ever we told them about it. Perhaps they might if Jim had hit it and we'd died in a horrible mangled collision of horseflesh and auto parts.

At least we didn't have an upholstery incident.

You Can't Toss An Eel In England, But You Can Go On A Camel

Every so often I take a look at the British Broadcasting Corporation's news to get a different angle on world events. When I did that the other day, I was flooded with stories that show things are not quite right between animals and people in England these days.

There is, of course, one simple explanation for the problem - it's England. We are, after all, talking about a country where the Prince married a woman with an uncanny similarity to Secretariat.

In one story I learned the annual conger cuddling tournament had been cancelled after complaints by a lone animal rights activist.

The tournament has raised thousands of pounds for the local lifeboat crews over the past thirty or forty years. It would seem to be something along the lines of a giant bowling or skittles game, with teams of fishermen as the pins and a twenty-five pound dead eel suspended from a rope as the ball. The teams take turns attempting to knock each other from platforms by hurling the giant dead eel at them.

This is called fun in England.

They've been doing it for over thirty years in the town of Lyme-Regis southwest of London. The fact that the town name sounds remarkably similar to a drink involving copious amounts of gin, might explain why the residents there are willing to hurl giant dead eels at one another.

Then again, it could just be because they are British.

Women in North America often complain about construction crews heckling them as they walk past. Apparently, British construction crews do not like having the roles reversed. No, British women are not ganging up to hurl rude comments at the workers. Apparently, the construction crew in question has had to seek protection from a band of heckling baboons.

Work is underway at the Knowsley Safari Park near Liverpool on a new enclosure for the baboons and other primates. It's one of those zoos where the animals roam freely and visitors drive through in their cars. To protect themselves from approximately 120 primate hecklers, the workers have installed an electric fence, thereby making them the only animals in the zoo that are effectively in a cage. I know several women who would agree it is a good place for construction workers.

These same baboons were also in the news for stealing World Cup flags from cars in the park, giving us one more similarity between baboons and British soccer fans.

Another recent BBC news item was about a farmer in the Goonhilly area of Cornwall. (Believe me; I couldn't make up a name like that). He has started offering camel treks across the Lizard. I thought it sounded like a way to get rid of small reptiles at first, but it turned out the Lizard is some sort of a peninsula.

I may have also missed something in the translation between English and English when I read that the farmer said, "Even people who usually ride horses want to experience going on a camel."

I used to have a neighbor who claimed that going on an anthill was better than any insecticide for getting rid of them, but I can't imagine anyone who would want to go on a camel. I should think the People for the Ethical Treatment of Animals would be jumping out of their plastic sandals at the thought.

My favorite recent animal story out of Dear Olde England was about a woman in London forced to remove a sign from her front lawn that says, "Our dogs are fed on Jehovah Witnesses."

She's had the sign for over thirty years after some Jehovah Witnesses knocked on her door on Christmas morning. Apparently someone did not like the idea of feeding members of a religious group to dogs.

Margo Bates tells the story in her very funny book, *PS. Don't Tell Your Mother*, about how her grandmother took shot at the local Jehovah Witness in a community in northern British Columbia, but even she wouldn't have fed him to her dogs.

I for one would never consider feeding my dog a Jehovah Witness.

I'd be afraid she'd never stop scratching at the front door.

Standing Up For Our Aims

A year or so ago I wrote a column about a product that had been invented to let women take care of a full bladder from a standing position. Ostensibly, it was for campers and hikers to make taking care of business easier out in the woods.

I heard from a lot of women after that column. Some wanted to know where they could get the product. Others who wanted to point out just how lucky men were because we don't have to deal with long line-ups at public facilities. One woman wrote to say how she wished she could go in and out of a public washroom in thirty seconds the way her husband did.

I didn't have the heart to tell her he probably wasn't stopping to wash his hands if he could do it that quickly.

I have often seen men stopped at the side of the road relieving the pressure in their bladders. A few days ago I spotted a man off to the side of the highway. What was odd about that sighting was that the man was driving a motor home, which one would think had an onboard washroom he could have used.

I have a bit of a phobia about doing that at the side of the road. It developed about ten years ago, when I was driving through the mountains in the middle of the night, miles from the nearest service station, and feeling the effects of the twenty-ounce coffee I bought at the start of the trip a couple of hours earlier.

I hadn't seen another car for fifteen or twenty minutes, so I felt reasonably safe pulling off to the side of the highway. As I stood by the shoulder, it became immediately clear I was not quite so alone on the road. Before I could finish a convoy of three chartered busses crested the hill. When the drivers spotted me, they all turned on their high beams, and honked repeatedly, letting me know I had been caught in the act, and signaling their passengers to look at the guy peeing at the side of the road.

I think the dogs painted on the side of the busses even barked a couple of times.

That was the last time I ever made a pit stop at the side of the road.

The fact of the matter is men and women have different abilities. I often get accused of chauvinism when I make a statement like that, but I think I am on fairly safe ground when discussing the ability to relieve oneself from a standing position.

Apparently, a Norwegian primary school headmistress does not want to let her young charges experience that subtle, yet important difference between the sexes.

According to a story that appeared in the Sunday Telegraph a couple of weeks ago, Anne Lise Gjul, the headmistress of a mixed primary school in the southern Norwegian city of Kristiansand, wants to introduce a measure banning boys from urinating while standing up. She brought this about after dealing with numerous complaints from the janitors that many of the male pupils can't aim properly.

The Norwegian media have discussed little else since. Why cover stories about war, the economy, or the rising price of pickled herring, when you can focus on seven-year-olds with bad aims.

In a letter to parents, she wrote, "Help. We have to wipe up a lot around the lavatory bowls and it's getting on our nerves. Discuss at home whether boys should sit down when they go for a pee."

The politicians couldn't resist tying their kites to a story getting that much press. Vidar Kleppe, the head of Norway's far-right Justice and Order party didn't disappoint.

"If boys are not allowed to pee in the natural way that they have done for generations, then it amounts to an assault on God's creations," he said.

Far be it from me to agree with far-right politicians, but men really do need to stand up for these poor young boys. Obviously, the headmistress doesn't know what everyone who has ever stopped at a service station restroom knows.

It's not just seven-year-olds who can't aim.

That's Really Cold Cash

It's been said that a great percentage of the North American population is hoping to be financially stable during their retirement years by winning the lottery. Their investment decisions are based on the tables in the back of The Racing Forum instead of the tables in the back of a blue-chip investment prospectus.

I am not immune to the lure of a lottery ticket. I've played the same six numbers in the lottery for the past twenty years. For a million dollars I will tell you what they are so you can avoid ever picking those numbers because they have returned almost $120.00 on my investment of $2600.00.

My wife is an investment broker. (They don't like the term stockbroker anymore, but if I told you why, she'd have to kill me.) She could make a lot more money if she wasn't working with the disability of having scruples. She doesn't take clients who want to turn a thousand dollars into a million between now and Christmas. She doesn't take clients who want to invest all their money in speculative penny stocks. She steers people away from overloading their portfolios with risky ventures and pie-in-the-sky investments. As a result we might not be as rich as the brokers to celebrities like Martha Stewart, but on the up side she can sleep at night and look herself in the mirror in the morning.

I think I may have found a way to earn a lot of money after I stop working. There's just one catch.

I'd have to die.

Forbes releases an annual list of dead people who earned over $5-million last year. If dead people can make that kind of money why, oh why, can't I?

Elvis Presley made $45-million last year. Of course there are those that would debate whether or not he is really dead. In some corners it's felt that he might actually be making even more money by working the counter at a Burger King on Mars. I saw him just the other day. He was on a billboard near my home advertising his newest collection of greatest hits.

Am I wrong, or have there been more collections of Presley's greatest hits than there were original Presley records?

Charles Shultz brought in a cool $35-million. Can you imagine how many nickels Lucy would have to collect at her psychiatry stand to make that much? While he wasn't, his cartoon characters have become immortal. I always find it a little ironic when I see Snoopy and the rest of the bunch being used as pitchmen for life insurance, when the guy who drew them no longer needs that product.

The time has come.
The time is now.
Dr. Seuss got ten million
He can't spend anyhow.

The image of Marilyn Monroe brought in $5-million. It was one thing to fantasize about her when she was alive, but whenever I see her picture I have to wonder just how many people would want to look at her in her birthday suit today, had she lived. Oh sure, cosmetic surgery can do a lot of wonderful things to the aging body, but Marilyn would be over eighty if she were alive today. Her birthday suit might need a good ironing.

I think she'd probably look a lot better under the bearskin rug.

Others on the list included John Lennon ($22-million), Andy Warhol ($16-million), and J.R.R. Tolkien ($8-million). George Harrison, Johnny Cash and Irving Berlin all earned $7-million from beyond the grave.

I don't expect my needs to be that great after I'm dead. I'm almost sure I could get by quite comfortably in the great beyond if I made a million or two each year. Since the combined earnings of the people on the Forbes list totaled $186-million, I think it would be a nice gesture if each of them sent me a few bucks to spend for them.

They probably wouldn't even feel it.

E-coli My New Best Friend

I knew it all along.

You can't say I haven't been warning you, but odds are there are still a lot who haven't listened. Now it's in the news, maybe you'll see just how prophetic my words were.

Vegetables are bad for you.

Bad. Bad. Bad. Bad. Bad.

Hundreds of people have become ill from eating e-coli laden spinach. They should have listened to me.

Over the years I have written several columns about the noxious substances that often occupy space on my plates. They take away room on the plate that would be better filled with good food; less e-coli coated vegetables and more spice-coated beer-marinated meat.

Of course, that statement will probably get me in trouble with PETA, the People for the Ethical Treatment Of Animals. On the other hand the other PETA will be in full agreement. The People Eating Tasty Animals love nothing more than a good slab of beef to dig into at mealtime.

As a child, my mother tried to serve me a wide variety of vegetable products. She pointed out that Popeye got his strength from spinach, something virtually every mother throughout the Fifties and Sixties tried to pass off as the truth, Even then, I knew Popeye was a two dimensional drawing, and therefore did not have taste buds. If he did, he would have been opening up a canned ham instead of a can of spinach.

When the news broke about the offending spinach packages, my son went to the refrigerator and discovered we had a package of something that looked like lawn clippings and dandelion leaves from the same company that had been cited as the source for the offending spinach. It was immediately dispatched to the garbage bin.

I can assure you, if you really need to be reassured, we did not have that botanical mishmash because of any purchase decisions on my part. That was my wife's doing.

I always knew one day she'd try to poison me with vegetables.

We used to be a reasonably sane couple, who shopped for meat, bread, and a few sensible vegetables like corn, peas and tomatoes. All that went out the window a few months back. I've had to learn the meaning of arugula, cilantro, and kale.

Frankly, I've pulled more appetizing looking vegetation out of a clogged lawnmower.

The sudden change in our dietary regimen was brought about by my wife's decision to lose weight. As any husband out there knows, there is one very clear rule to life:

When Mama makes a decision, we all make the same decision.

Diane's decision to eat a more balanced diet, is leaving me feeling a little unbalanced. OK, I know. I'm a little unbalanced at the best of times, but you're all used to that. I've often admitted to being big for my age, and much of that is due to a daily intake of as unbalanced a diet as I can ingest.

As a result, I am losing a bit of weight, too. It only stands to reason, that if we no longer have any of the fun but unbalanced foods in the house, I won't be able to eat them either. Even if we go out to eat, I am forced to consider the healthy alternative, because, should I decide to order a bacon double cheese burger I will get one of those withering looks that wives can do so well.

I'm already withered enough, thank you very much.

I haven't seen the inside of a donut in over three months. I'm beginning to show signs of withdrawal. The three closest donut shops to my home have had to lay off staff.

Living with a spouse who is determined to shed extra poundage is a little like living with someone who has just quit smoking or drinking. You've all been around people like that. They are more than happy to tell you about all the reasons you should not partake in the product selections they would have willing joined you in consuming just a few weeks ago.

But now thanks to a minute little microbe, I won't be seeing any spinach on my plates for the foreseeable future.

Bordering On A Traffic Jam

There are four border crossings between the United States and Canada in my immediate vicinity. Last weekend, all four of them were effectively closed.

It wasn't that Congressman Charlie Norwood (R-Georgia) had finally gotten his wish to have 12,000 armed National Guardsmen patrolling the border, protecting America from wandering bands of metric converters, hockey fans and figure skaters. In fact it wasn't even an American decision to close the border.

On the afternoon of Sunday September 24, 2006, US Homeland Security advised Canadian officials that an armed fugitive wanted on a homicide warrant in California might be heading to Canada through one of those four crossings. As a result, the Canadian Customs officers did exactly what you or I might have done if we had been told an armed and dangerous fugitive was planning to stop by our workplace.

They left early.

Thousands of cars and commercial trucks cross at those four entry points every day. I'm often one of them.

I keep a mailbox in the small town of Sumas, Washington. It speeds up the delivery of my mail from American sources, and cuts the cost of my magazine subscriptions. Diane and I often do go down there on a Sunday to pick up the mail and shop. Thankfully, though, with everything going on around selling our home, we did not made the trip south that day. If we had, we would have found ourselves sitting in a traffic tie-up that stretched for miles into the United States. It got to the point that the cues for two of the crossings actually merged.

Probably the only positive note the drivers could think about while the hours ticked by, was that the gas they were burning was undoubtedly purchased in the United States for a lot less than they would have paid for it in Canada.

I'm sure they weren't thinking too many positive things about the Canadian Customs guards.

In defense of the customs guards, I have to say there is a certain justification for their actions. Canadian border guards, like Canadians in general, are unarmed. While I am generally not in favor of anyone in my immediate vicinity carrying a loaded weapon, I realize that with all they have to potentially face in their jobs, border guards might need to have a sidearm at their disposal.

Somehow, I don't think it would bring any degree of fear into the heart of an armed and dangerous fugitive, if a Canadian border guard shouted, "Stop, or I'll throw my ballpoint pen at you."

It just doesn't have the same ring to it as, "Stop, or I'll shoot," does it?

American border guards are armed. As a result, when I am heading south I always make sure there is nothing in my possession that might make them wish to take their guns out of their holsters. Even my dog knows that when we are heading to the border there will be no contraband, potentially mad cow infected dog biscuits in the car. She's OK with that, although I think she'd like the male chocolate Labrador that works there to come over and sniff around just to be sure.

While I see the need for the guards to be armed, I'm just not sure all of the ones I come into contact with should be given a weapon. Most are quite capable of handling the responsibility.

Most, not all.

I'm glad one in particular didn't have a weapon when he searched my car a few years ago. In doing so he found the small bag I carry with me containing medical supplies I need to deal with my disability. He thought he'd found a mother lode of drug paraphernalia. He pulled a urinary catheter from the bag and demanded to know what it was. I gave him a detailed account of what it did and how and where it gets inserted. By the time I finished his knees were starting to buckle.

I think if he'd had a weapon he might have used it on me to get me to stop the description, or on himself to get the image out of his mind.

Cn U Rd Dis, I Nu U Cud

From time to time, I hear my father's words coming from my mouth. It's usually pretty disturbing.

It happened again a couple of days ago, when an Associated Press news item crossed my desk with the headline, "Officials: Students can use 'text speak' on tests."

OK, it wasn't an immediate reaction. First, I had to find out that text speak wasn't some new schoolbook with an audio feature. For those of you who are similarly behind the times, text speak is a form of spelling used when text messaging. Apparently vowels and grammar are optional.

As the news item said, "Text-speak, a second language for thousands of teens, uses abbreviated words and phrases such as "txt" for "text", "lol" for "laughing out loud" or "lots of love," and "CU" for "see you."

Kids today have it so easy. There they are. My father's words coming out of me. Like many of his words, they leave me with a question or two.

4 xmpl wr ws txt spk wn I wz in skl?

In text speak, the answer to the question 'What did Lincoln say at Gettysburg' would be, "4 scr + 7 yrs ago, r fthrs brot 4th on dis contnt a nw nashn."

Had Lincoln looked at the paper in his hand and seen those words, I'm sure he would have turned to one of his aides and uttered the immortal words, "Can I buy a vowel?"

I might have even been able to pass French if I didn't have to worry about how I spelled ou est le stylo de ma tante.

Spelling wasn't optional in my elementary school classrooms in the nineteen-sixties, but now in the twenty-first century, students in New Zealand need not worry about it. New Zealand's Qualifications Authority said that it still strongly discourages students from using anything other than full English, but that credit will be given if the answer "clearly shows the required understanding," even if it contains text speak.

Or perhaps I should say, Nu Zlands Kwalfcashuns Athrty sed dat it stil strngly dscrages studnts frm uzn n e thing othr thn full eng, bt dat credit wil b given f d ans "clearly shoz d req'd undrstndn," evn f it contanz text-speak.

I had elementary school teachers who quite literally believed a spelling mistake was grounds for corporal punishment, and one who I am convinced thought it might be a capital offence. I can still feel the sharp rap of her ruler across my knuckles whenever I accidentally misspelled a word.

I have written before about the mail I get from my fellow Canadians who read this column and feel compelled to write. They complain that I use Webster's dictionary spelling instead of Oxford. Because this column appears in more American newspapers than Canadian, it will always have words like color, flavor, and neighbor instead of colour, flavour and neighbour.

I'm sure that ruler-wielding elementary school teacher would be among them if she were able to get the column where she is now. I'd like to think a small demon is repeatedly rapping her across the knuckles down there.

Obviously language changes over time. New words come and go. What is yours today was 'thine' a few hundred years ago. A shop today might have been called a shoppe in Dickens' time.

But what if Shakespeare had written in text speak.

Richard the Third could have implored all his online buddies for "a hors a hors my kngdm 4 a hors."

The witches in Macbeth could have text messaged each other the words of their hex as, "2X 2X toil n trubl. Fire brn n cldrn bbl"

Julius Caesar could have sent a message to Brutus that would simply have said, "A 2", to which Brutus could have replied, "C U, LOL."

I can't see myself using text speak to write my columns or books. My word processing programs underlines everything that it thinks is a spelling error with a red line, and right now my screen looks like something out of one of those Texas Chainsaw Massacre movies. I think the software might be internally hemorrhaging.

N f I did 2 mny editrs wud go blistic.

You Can Take Me Anywhere, You Just Can't Dress Me Up

I've never been what you might call a dedicated follower of fashion. Working from home allows me the privilege of not having to wear a suit to the office. I avoid ties with my undivided attention. As far as I am concerned, wearing jeans and a clean sweatshirt is getting dressed up.

Let's not even talk about tuxedoes.

I've worn cowboy boots when they were in fashion and when they weren't. I have always enjoyed the comfort a good pair of cowboy boots brings. After I broke my spine, doctors thought it would be a good idea if I switched to a special type of orthopedic shoe. One day I tried on one of my old pairs of boots and discovered that, not only were they a lot better looking, but they acted like braces on the lower part of my legs, and made walking with my crutches a whole lot easier.

I don't wear jewelry, with the exception of my wedding ring, a Navaho ring, and a small gold stud in my left earlobe. The pierced ear might be a sign that I am trying to be fashionable, but it's not. And, yes, before you ask, it is in the correct ear to indicate my heterosexuality.

I got it when I thought my sons were reaching the age when they might consider getting a variety of locations on their bodies pierced. By sacrificing my own ear before they had a chance, I knew I would never have to worry about coming to the breakfast table and seeing my sons with enough rings across their eyebrows to hang a shower curtain. No self-respecting teenager is ever going to get anything pierced after his father has already done it.

It worked like a charm. It's been there for more than ten years, and neither of my sons have a single piercing.

As it is, the boys have always been quite disgusted with my sense of style. They've never had any qualms about telling me I need a haircut. It's the same thing father said through much of the late Sixties and early Seventies. At least they can rest assured that I am not going to embarrass them any further by following the latest fashion advice for men coming out of New York.

I sat in horror the other day, watching a news report about a growing trend in men's fashion. I cannot imagine ever falling victim to this latest trend, and I hope you all appreciate it.

I will not wear one in a van.
I will not wear one on the can.
No red, or blue, or green, or tan,
Dresses for me,
Because I'm a man.
That's right, dresses.
Dresses for men.

They weren't talking about dresses for men who like to dress up like women. The fashion show that was reported on the news displayed dresses for men at the office, dresses for men to wear on casual occasions, and dresses for formal wear.

They cited great historical precedence for the custom of dressing a man like Ken when he secretly sneaks into Barbie's dream home closets. The Romans, Greeks, Egyptians and Scots all wore dress and skirt-like apparel. Bad examples - three long-gone civilizations and a bunch of guys who *'ya ca' nay hardly oonderstand a word they're sayin' 'cuz they're freezin' their frickin' buttocks off in a skirt, Laddie.*

The dresses in the fashion show ranged from something that looked like Scarlet O'Hara in her curtain-wearing phase, to mini-skirts. One looked like something that might be accessorized with a pointy hood and a burning cross.

I give great credit to women for being able to function in a dress. Men wouldn't even know how to sit properly. I can't imagine trying to get out of a car, while maintaining any sense of decency or decorum.

I guess the closest I have ever come to wearing a dress would be on those occasions when I have been forced to wear a hospital gown. At six-foot, four inches, a hospital gown leaves more of me uncovered than covered, and that's not even taking into consideration the sweeping open back.

If I had ever wondered, one look in a mirror would have told me I really don't have the physical attributes needed to properly carry off this dress-wearing thing.

On the other hand, if tent wearing ever comes into style, I'll be a natural for the role as spokes-model.

And You Thought You Had Trouble Keeping Names Straight

I read a news report about a man in Utah who was charged with polygamy. He and his five current wives live in a collection of battered mobile homes in Utah. All six of them claim to be living happily together with their twenty-nine children. That doesn't even include an additional five ex-wives, two of whom are the mothers of two of his current wives. Confused? Don't worry so am I.

This report begs a number of questions. First and foremost has to be, "What the heck was he thinking?" This isn't a family. It's a village.

Apparently the family supports itself by selling magazine subscriptions by telephone. That's reason enough for me to dislike them. I get at least one call a week from someone trying to sell me magazines I already subscribe to, as well as several I have no particular interest in reading. While I bet they could be fairly persuasive salespeople for Brides magazine, I'm not so sure they could relate as well to Cooking For Two.

There's an old joke about the biggest deterrent from bigamy being the fact it comes with two mothers-in-law. I can't even begin to imagine having three (his wives include two sets of sisters) plus the five ex-mothers-in-law. Let's face it, though. This guy has to be a bear for punishment. The stress of having at least one wife suffering from PMS at any given point in time would probably cause an ordinary man to develop, or at least pray for, a cerebral aneurysm.

One of the wives is referred to as the "head wife" (No, I'm not going to go off on the tangent that job title conjures up. Some jokes just write themselves, don't they?) Her job is to keep everything organized, including deciding which wife gets to sleep in the husband's trailer each night. Since he's between twenty and thirty years older than the women, I'd have to wonder if the sleeping arrangements are decided by a reward system or if they are a punishment for not selling enough magazine subscriptions.

At least he only has to get dressed with one wife each morning. There are only so many ways you can say, "No that outfit doesn't make you look fat" before you start to get bored by your own repetitiveness. I also have to give him a bit of credit for avoiding one other potential problem. Each wife has her own trailer home. If he hadn't thought to do that, he'd spend half his life refereeing the who-gets-to-control-the-thermostat tournament.

With twenty-nine children between the ages of two and fourteen, plus four pregnant wives, his grocery and pharmacy bill each month must look like the gross national product of several Third World countries. I had enough trouble dealing with two sons and their constant refrain of, "Is there anything to eat around here?" I thought they consumed enough to keep our local Costco outlet in business. This guy probably keeps the whole chain afloat. Just how many magazine subscription sales does it take to cover their peanut butter consumption costs let alone the additional expenses for jam and bread?

He still has a couple of years before his offspring start wanting to borrow the family car, but when it starts he'll need to get a fleet discount at several car dealerships, and a real boost in the sales of Popular Mechanics subscriptions.

The newspaper report didn't mention anything about how the children feel about being a part of this arrangement. It's one thing to believe that your mother always loved your siblings best, but can you imagine going through life with the feeling that five moms loved the other twenty-eight of your siblings best.

Somehow I think there might be a whole mess of therapy in their futures.

Apparently this isn't all that unusual a situation in Utah. Despite banning the practice in 1896 as a condition for statehood, it's estimated there are at least 30,000 covert polygamists in the state.

The guy is facing up to twenty-five years in jail on the four polygamy counts. There's also a separate charge of child rape thrown in for good measure, because he was thirty-eight and his oldest wife was just thirteen when she became pregnant with their first.

In a way, for his sake, I hope they throw the book at him. He could probably use the rest, and he'll probably miss that period when he'd have to answer all five wives asking him, "Is it hot in here or is it just me?"

I just wonder how many license plates he'll have to make before he can afford a subscription to Family Fun magazine.

Reason #58 For Not Keeping A Sledge Hammer In The Bathroom

OK. Now I'm scared.

As a husband, it's only natural that from time to time (OK, a lot) I will forget to replace a roll of toilet paper, or fail to return a toilet seat from its more convenient up position to the down setting preferred by the female member of the household.

I think I'm going to have to be a whole lot more careful about these things in the future, especially after Diane found out about Miami resident Franklin Paul Crowe's recent actions. I don't want her to follow his lead.

Crow was arrested recently and charged with the murder of his roommate. Apparently, he took a sledge hammer to the man's skull, as a permanent way of expressing his displeasure about empty toilet paper rolls. He beat the man so severely he could only be identified through fingerprint analysis.

Hitting someone over the head ten times with a sledge hammer because of an empty toilet paper roll would tend to rearrange facial features somewhat.

I can only imagine what he would have done if someone failed to flush.

One of my mother's euphemisms for the bathroom was 'the room where Lizzie Borden hid her ax.' Perhaps Lizzie's parents failed to replace whatever passed for toilet paper back then.

I really don't have any excuse for leaving the roll empty and, for that matter, no one around here needs to worry about being stranded by an empty roll. One of the tricks that Tara, my assistance dog performs exceedingly well is rescuing stranded toilet users by bringing them a fresh roll on command.

It's not as spectacular as letting Pa know that Timmy is stuck in the well again, but you have to admit, it's a pretty useful trick.

Reading the news item about Mr. Crow's inappropriate hammer use brought to mind a number of things that annoy me about toilets and toilet paper.

For example, I have a familial issue with toilet paper - not toilet paper in general, but a specific brand. The giant grocery warehouse chain Costco started marketing their own product lines several years ago, using the trade name Kirkland Signature. I have to admit that I thought it was neat when I saw the first product bearing my name, which was, as I recall, Kirkland Signature coffee. Our home is now filled with Kirkland Signature products ranging from shampoo to fabric softener. My dog even sleeps on a Kirkland Signature dog bed.

But I must say, the association of my surname with their products lost its luster when they brought out Kirkland Signature toilet paper.

Well, would you like your name tied to a product with that particular end use?

Our oldest son returned to the empty nest so that he could live free in the Mom & Dad bed and breakfast while he goes to school. His return produced some bathroom related issues. For example, I'm amazed that at his age, he actually seems to believe that if he clogs the toilet, the plunger fairy will come along and take care of it. He's also convinced that the wipe the floor around the toilet fairy visits to our house. I guess I shouldn't find that too hard to believe. After all, he seems to be convinced that we are regularly visited by the dishwashing fairy, the pick up after him fairy, the refrigerator filling fairy, and the spilled food and drink wipe-up fairy.

It's not enough to make me go looking for a sledge hammer to try to make my annoyance understood, but if I have to take on any more fairy roles around here, I'm going to sprout wings.

I might be more willing to head to the toolbox for a hammer if I ever meet the guy who came up the worst thing to hit public washroom stalls since the tiny single sheet toilet paper dispenser was invented.

Automatic flushing toilets.

I'm sure I'm not the only person who has ever moved the wrong way on the seat and received an unexpected icy colorectal shower due to an unplanned flush. It can be especially embarrassing if someone walks in while you are trying to dry yourself off with the electric air dryer.

But that's another story.

Down The Road Again

Supersized In A Small World

There's been a lot of talk over the past few years about the growth in North Americans, It's not about the quantity of people. It's about the quantity of cells in each person. Being big for my age, I have always been one leading the trend.

You would think that with all of this expansion going on, companies would consider it when designing their products and services. My experience this past weekend certainly made it clear airlines have not seen the change in passenger size as a reason to make their seats and aisles roomier. In fact, they have made them smaller.

If that trend continues, I am going to have to start coating my pants with petroleum jelly to make it easier to slide in between the armrests on plane seats.

While I admit to being big, I am not anywhere near the behemoth size of some of my traveling companions. One woman got on my flight from Seattle to Detroit last week and I swear I saw the plane tilt towards the door when she waddled aboard.

It was a four-hour flight spent sharing a row of three seats with two other travelers, one of whom was wider across the beam than I am. I had the aisle seat, the wider load had the center seat and a poor skinny little runt was crammed into the window seat.

I think he might have been begging for help from the flight attendants, but the sound coming from his seat was quite muffled.

In order to accommodate the three of us in the row, I lifted the armrest on the aisle side, and spent the flight perched precariously on the edge of my seat. That meant I was an easy target for everyone getting on and off the plane, and the flight attendants manning the beverage carts.

I knew I was in for a long hard flight. Even on the best of flights there is an FAA requirement that I will be hit in the head at least three times by backpacks belonging to passengers who have no idea how far the things protrude from their bodies. Add to that the fact that at least one child being carried down the aisle will kick me as he or she tries to wiggle out of the parent's arms.

It's a wonder I don't have a concussion after every flight.

As little comfort as the width, or rather lack of width, the seats offered, that was not the only problem I faced. The distance between the back of the seatback in front of me and the front of the seatback I was resting against was several inches less than my legs needed. That was further reduced by the woman seated in front of me, who insisted on attempting to recline her seat.

Repeatedly.

She wasn't successful, but she very nearly succeeded at relocating my knee joints to somewhere just a little south of my hips.

Body size isn't the only thing that is becoming supersized on flights lately. I'm always amazed by the number of people who seem to believe that the rule concerning the size of one's carry-on luggage applies to everyone but them. At least one person on every flight I have made in the past twelve months has delayed the boarding of the passengers behind them while they try to cram a twenty-inch wide suitcase into a fourteen-inch high overhead compartment.

Because I was going to be driving for four hours to Dayton, Ohio after I landed in Detroit I wanted a comfortable car that would handle the road in the event of a late winter or early spring snowstorm. I selected what I thought was a mid-sized sport utility vehicle – smaller than a Hum-V but bigger than most cars on the road. At least it looked bigger. The last time I had that little leg room in a car, I was four years old and trying to drive a neighbor's pedal car.

Even then, I was big for my age, and I've been suffering for it ever since.

All The Little Airlines Go Cheap, Cheap, Cheap

As I have said before, flying is not one of my favorite activities. I discovered a new reason for concern in the wild blue yonder recently, when I flew for the first time on a discount airline.

When your ticket is roughly half the price of the fare on the more well known airlines, you start to wonder how they cut the price, especially since the other airlines are all awash in red ink even with their higher prices. There are a few obvious clues and some that don't become apparent until you're airborne and it's too late to do anything about your predicament.

Meal and bar service hasn't completely disappeared, but it no longer includes the word, "complimentary." Since my return flight straddled the lunch hour, I decided that $5.00 for a ham and cheese sandwich wasn't too much to pay to fend off starvation. The sandwich answered the question about what happens to the sandwiches that sit around in the mini-marts at gas stations past their expiry dates.

The bread was dry enough to clean the tartar from the teeth of a gorilla.

...a very old gorilla.

When John Glenn was sitting in his Mercury capsule on the launch pad, he had a disquieting thought. Just before the end of the countdown he realized that everything used to build the rocket had been purchased from the lowest bidder. As my no-frills plane rumbled down the runway on its takeoff last week, I had the same thought about it.

I'm not sure about the wisdom of dropping the seat-pocket reading material, audio entertainment, and the movie. At least those things keep the passengers' minds off unsettling thoughts for part of the flight.

Free alcohol usually goes a long way to taking care of them for the rest of the flight.

Flight attendants are always insisting that your seat backs return to their upright position during take-off and landing. On both my outgoing and return flights this week, my seat back would return to its upright position, and then slowly recline by about fifteen degrees. This gave me something to think about other than wondering how much tread remained on the landing gear tires. Staring straight at the overhead bin above me got me wondering how much weight the other passengers had deposited directly above me, and how strong the latches were on the compartments.

When you walk on crutches, as I do, you get to board the aircraft ahead of the other passengers. This gives me time to get to my seat before everyone else stampedes down the ramp like a heard of sheep heading for the meat packers. Occasionally it also makes me privy to information I would rather not have. On my recent flight two flight attendants were standing on seats looking at the oxygen bottle in the first overhead compartment.

"I can't tell," said one.

"I'm not sure either," added the other, "but it probably doesn't really matter whether it's expired or not."

I knew it.

All those flight attendant speeches I've listened to over the years were just one big lie, made up to lull passengers into a false sense of security and to think there really is safety equipment on board that gives them a chance to survive an in-flight emergency.

On this flight, that little speech seemed to go a lot faster than I remembered from other airlines. It didn't dawn on me until I looked out the window at the cold, gray waters of Lake Huron and Lake Superior what had been left out. There was no mention of life preservers or seat bottoms that can double as floatation devices. If we go down in water we don't need them, because, let's face it, an airliner full of passengers and baggage isn't going to float long enough to make them of any use. The discount airlines must be saving a fortune by not bothering to pacify their customers about the end result of a water landing.

In a way, you could say flying a discount airline was a bit of a religious experience. I'm sure there were a lot of prayers being said as the plane shook its way through turbulence.

I even considered emulating the Pope.

When I got off the plane I thought about bending down and kissing the ground the way he does. Then my stomach reminded me about that sandwich and I thought it would be safest to avoid bending for a while.

Oklahoma – It's A Learning Experience

I always learn something new when I go to Oklahoma. That might surprise some people, especially those who've had their image of the state set by Merle Haggard's song, Okie From Muskogee.

Last year, when my appearance tour made a stop in Oklahoma City I learned about noodling. That's the art of using your fingers as catfish bait. It's also a good way to inadvertently catch a beaver or a water moccasin.

Last week went to Oklahoma for more appearances and to further my education in all things Southern.

Culinary delights are often a learning experience for me. As most of my regular readers know only too well, there are certain items I firmly believe should not, under any circumstances, ever pass between my lips. That list is topped by broccoli and anything else that smells like a gorilla's armpit.

That's not to say that I am not adventurous when it comes to trying new foods. In The Philippines, I ate balut; a semi-cooked duck egg with the duckling ready to hatch.

I ate it. I didn't retain it. The bird managed to fly back up the way it went in.

In Oklahoma City, one meal included alligator. I have to assume they moved north after Hurricane Katrina, because I don't remember reading about any great Oklahoma alligator drives in my history textbooks in school.

Believe it or not, alligator doesn't taste like chicken.

I was also served okra. People in Oklahoma were surprised I had never eaten okra before. They didn't realize I generally limit my vegetable intake to whatever can be found in a Caesar salad, peas, corn, and the hops, barley and wheat in beer.

Believe it or not, okra does not taste like chicken either.

Anytime that I travel south of the Mason-Dixon Line, I am reminded I speak with an accent. Apparently, my impression that the residents of that geographic region speak with an accent is mistaken.

If I use the words out, about or house in a sentence, I can be guaranteed someone will snicker and try to imitate the way

I say them. This week in Oklahoma, I mentioned something that included all three in the sentence, "It was about the size of an outhouse."

Three people passed beer through their noses when I said that.

It can be very distracting for a comedian, when a sentence like that, in the middle of your material, gets a bigger laugh than the punch line.

I also learn new words and phrases when I am on tour. This week I learned the word, "tetched."

It was used in the sentence, "My whole family is tetched."

Don't bother looking it up in your copy of Webster's. It won't be there. As near as I can determine, it is a little like being touched, but with an important difference.

If you are touched, it is an unfortunate thing that cannot be helped. You are just a little touched. You'll ride the short school bus, and possibly spend your life wearing a hockey helmet.

If you are tetched, you are just as 'special,' but you could probably prevent it. Someone who is tetched might show his or her displeasure by firing a rifle so the bullet misses, but comes close enough that you need to change your underwear. As I was told, a woman who is tetched might be inclined to smack her husband with a cast iron skillet; not the new cheap thin ones, but one of the big old heavy ones, preferably filled with hot okra.

Clearly, you do not want to tick off someone who is tetched.

I also think you'd have to be a bit tetched to go noodling.

As I was flying home from Oklahoma City, I saw several people on my flight who were tetched. Two of them were flight attendants.

When I received my meal on the plane, I was reminded of the lovely meal of alligator and okra I had eaten just a couple of days before. The airline meal included a hot chicken sandwich. I only know that because I read the label in the wrapper.

It didn't taste like chicken either.

Pssst... Wanna Buy A Hot Week

Diane and I attended my niece's wedding on the weekend. It was a learning experience.

It wasn't the wedding itself that was educational, although for a moment, when the groom arrived at the front of the church wearing a kilt, I thought I might be witnessing my first same-sex marriage.

Our accommodations for the weekend taught us the value of booking a hotel early and spending whatever it costs, even if a 'free' room is available.

My niece is the co-host of a morning radio show in a small city a couple of hundred miles from our home. Set on the side of a large lake in an area that sees very good weather for much of the year, the city is very attractive to tourists. As a result, there was no room in the inns.

One of Diane's friends had given us a pamphlet offering three free nights in a resort in that city. In return, we had to attend a meeting with the resort owners to hear the benefits of owning a timeshare there.

It sounded painless; two hours of touring the resort's golf course, riding stables, and accommodations. I should have known better. I am a living, breathing example of someone who too quickly forgets the old adage, if it sounds too good to be true...

Any of you who have ever experienced the sales pitch for a timeshare resort are probably nodding your heads as you read this. So many things are more enjoyable than spending two hours with a timeshare salesperson.

It's close, but I would have to say it was not quite as much fun as a colonoscopy. In this case, timeshare ownership was being shoved down my throat. In the colonoscopy, something was being shoved somewhere else, but at least no salesperson was involved.

We started the meeting by making it clear that, while we thought the resort was very nice, we would not be making a purchase. We were willing to hear what the program involved and tour the resort, but we were not buying a week there for the next forty years.

At least I thought the words, "We won't be purchasing anything today" were pretty clear when they left my mouth. Apparently, they were not quite as clear when they reached her ears.

Still, no matter how unpleasant the experience was about to be, we knew it was only going to last two hours.

Yeah. Right.

We rode around the resort on a golf cart. I've never found it that difficult to drive a golf cart, but the salesperson drove with all the skill of a sixteen-year-old learning to drive a car with a manual transmission. I hadn't experienced that many jerks since I accidentally accepted a booking to speak to a group of tax collectors.

We returned to the office almost two hours after the meeting began. Diane and I were past being ready to head out to lunch, but the salesperson was just getting wound up. Not wishing to be impolite, but thinking of nothing other than lunch, we sat through her spiel of incentives she was willing to offer us for signing a contract that day.

As the two-hour meeting approached its third hour, and my stomach started making noises like a Siberian tiger that hadn't eaten a villager in three or four weeks. We knew the concept of not making a purchase hadn't gotten through.

We repeated, "We won't be purchasing anything today"

In any other business communication that would normally end the meeting. When it became clear the salesperson was not getting a pen to connect with our checkbook, the sales manager came out of his office.

I now know what happens to salespeople who are too sleazy to be used car salesmen at those lots that sell the cars insurance companies have written off as beyond potential repair. They become sales managers at timeshare resorts.

The next time we have to visit a city that has no room at the inn, I'll seek out the closest stable. At least, no one will try to sell me a week in a manger for the next forty years.

I Have My Own Air Terror

I've mentioned before that I do not find flying to be one of my favorite activities. I wouldn't go so far as to say I am a white-knuckle flyer, but I do tend to lose some of the color from my finger joints during take-offs and landings.

When we are aloft, I am fine and usually fall asleep within a few minutes, depending on how long it takes to get my heart rate back to normal after the takeoff.

You'd think I'd be used to it by now. In the past six weeks, I have made eight cross country flights. It's flights like the last two that seem to keep me from ever becoming used to it.

A few days ago I took off from Seattle, heading to Washington, DC. It was an overnight flight, leaving at eleven o'clock at night and arriving in DC at six-thirty the next morning. The takeoff was smooth and it wasn't long before I was nodding off.

I heard a woman's voice saying, "Sir. You aren't allowed to sleep."

I assumed it was just part of a dream, but a few seconds later she repeated it. I slid my eyes open just enough to see that the voice was not coming from a dream maiden who wanted to have her way with me on the flight, but it was the flight attendant leaning over me demanding I stay awake.

"Why can't I sleep?" I asked her.

"Not you," she said. "The man beside you is armed and he can't fall asleep during the flight."

If that won't propel you into a full blown a wide-awake state I don't know what will. There was no way I was going to nod off, knowing the man beside me was armed. Especially since he showed no signs of waking up. What if he was startled, and went into one of those semi-conscious rampages you read about?

When the man finally stirred, he told the flight attendant that he was not on duty, was not a federal air marshal, but as an FBI agent needed to have his weapon with him. He didn't plan to use it, and he wanted to go to sleep.

The flight attendant was not going to give in. She told him it was an airline regulation that all armed passengers must stay awake throughout the entire flight.

I wonder if that includes terrorists.

The end result was I was fully awake and stayed that way through the entire flight, which, in the end, let me see just how close I would be coming to a being an unwilling participant in a major air disaster.

As we approached Dulles Airport outside Washington, we were on a course for a smooth landing. I still dug my fingernails into the armrests just to be on the safe side. We crossed the fence line around the airport and were about thirty feet above the runway when the plane suddenly shuddered and started back up. The sudden change in direction and the shaking of the plane woke the remaining passengers, many of whom screamed loudly. A puddle started forming under the passenger across the aisle from me, and I am almost certain the same thing was happening in the cockpit.

Apparently, at the last moment before landing, a plane on the ground had ventured onto our runway. Our pilot was forced to take evasive action. The alternative would have been very messy.

I have to assume the problem came from improper directions from the tower. It would have been a bit of synchronicity if we had been landing at Washington's other airport; the one named after the president who fired all the air traffic controllers in the 1980's.

One of my colleagues in Washington said I should be safe getting on a plane now that I have had my close call with disaster. I should have known better that to take his reassurances.

On my return flight to Seattle I became a passenger with the puddle forming under my seat.

A flight attendant held a tray of orange juice and ice-water over my lap to offer it to my seatmates.

That's when the turbulence hit.

I'm Headed For Dayton And I'm Actually Happy About It

I'm on my way to beautiful downtown Dayton, Ohio.

Dayton may not come to mind when thinking about exciting places to visit. Their visitor's bureau calls the city the birthplace of aviation, because it was home to the Wright Brother's bicycle shop, but even Wilbur and Orville decided North Carolina seemed like a better place to go flying.

The founding fathers of the city didn't name the river that flows through town the Dayton River. For some reason, it's the Miami River. Somehow, I don't expect to see too many beach bunnies sunning themselves along its shores in March. Perhaps they just wanted to feel a kinship with Florida during those long, cold Ohio winters.

I'll have to be on good behavior in Dayton. I won't be able to make any comments about the noxious substance that often appear on my plates at banquets. In their wisdom, Ohio legislators banned making disparaging remarks about produce several years ago. As a result, George Bush Senior and I cannot let our feelings about broccoli become a topic of conversation in Ohio.

Still, I'm excited about going to Dayton, because it is also home to an event honoring the woman who made it possible for people like me to have careers. This week, the University of Dayton hosts the Erma Bombeck Writer's Workshop. Erma spent decades writing about the humor in day to day life, before her untimely passing. Just about everyone in this business points to her as an inspiration.

Those who don't haven't learned where to give credit when it's due. No one did more for humor writing than Erma.

One of the greatest honors in my career has been the invitation two years ago to join the faculty the Workshop, something that no other Canadian writer can lay claim to.

The Workshop gives me a chance to thank Erma's widower Bill, their daughter Betsy, and sons Andrew and Matt for sharing her with the rest of us for so many years. Betsy, Andrew and Matt can probably sympathize with my sons for growing up with people reading about their exploits in a weekly newspaper column. As my son Brad says, "I'll probably discuss it with a therapist at some future date."

This year I will be presenting one of the keynote speeches, along with another person who prefers this type of work to serious writing, Pulitzer Prize winning columnist, Dave Barry. Actually, I don't think either of us is capable of serious writing.

It will be fun getting the chance to work with Dave. I owe him a drink or twelve because he wrote one of the cover comments for my new book, *I Think I'm Having One Of Those Decades*. The book will be having its official launch at the Workshop.

Dave said, "Canada has given the United States many wonderful gifts: Beer. Hockey. That famous entertainer, whatshisname. Beer. The list goes on and on. And to this list we must add the name of Gordon Kirkland, a very funny writer who is able to find humor in just about anything, because the only alternative would be for him to get a real job. As a fellow class clown suffering from maturity impairment, I salute him."

If anyone knows about maturity impairment, it's Dave.

OK, I'm pretty familiar with it, too.

This week also marks an event that might indicate that I have finally arrived in my own country. In many areas - and in comedy in particular - it seems that Canadians don't recognize their own until they become known somewhere else. That's one of the reasons comedy is one of my country's biggest exports; falling just short of marijuana and same-sex marriage licenses.

For years, my column has run in more American papers than Canadian. I'm invited to speak and perform at numerous events in the United States, but few at home.

But that may be changing. The Canadian edition of Reader's Digest magazine hits the stands this week. Included this month is a feature article about me. Suddenly seven million Canadian readers will find out about me.

That should be a shock to their systems.

Frankly, it's a bit of a shock to mine.

I just wish Erma was still here to see it.

My Country 'Tis Of The True North Strong And Free, Eh?

Like a lot of other Canadian writers and entertainers, I looked at a map of North America one day and said, "Gee, I wonder what the green blob is under the pink thing."

Over the last several years I've found numerous outlets for my writing in American publications. For some reason many of them have been in the Deep South. (My sons think it has something to do with me being a redneck.) I spend a lot of time touring in the United States promoting my books and newspaper column.

Some people think that means I've sold out – abandoned my country in pursuit of American dollars. OK, so I like getting paid in dollars that are worth a buck fifteen up here. I liked it even better when an American dollar was worth a buck and a half Canadian.

I believe it is my duty to teach Americans a thing or two about their northern neighbors. Surprisingly, the differences between us are of interest to Americans as well. The topic has come up just about every time I've appeared on radio or TV down there.

Canadians are familiar with stories about Americans arriving at the border in July with snow skis, parkas, and expecting to see us all living in igloos. We have to take a certain amount of the blame for that misconception. Personally, I blame the metric system, but then I blame it for many things, like no longer having any clue how to figure out the gas consumption of my car.

One of the major differences between us I try to point out to Americans is the fact that, in general, we are not nearly as well armed as they are. Many people down there are surprised when I tell them I do not own a gun, and that the only time I ever fired one it just about blew my right shoulder out of its socket because no one told me you weren't supposed to pull both triggers on a double-barreled shotgun at the same time.

Canada doesn't jump to the forefront in the minds of most Americans when discussing world powers. They tend to look at us as something like the Swiss Army, but without the really cool knife. I do my best to dispel this blatantly inaccurate stereotype. It isn't easy when so many people down there, especially many of the people in the media, are aware that the West Edmonton Mall has more submarines than our navy.

Even so, I take it as my personal responsibility to promote our strengths. In our defense I often point out Canada's important role saving the United States from nuclear annihilation during the Cold War. Few Americans know that the Soviet Union was incapable of firing intercontinental ballistic missiles at the United States because we were in the middle. I'm sure Khrushchev and Brezhnev often woke up with plans to bomb the United States only to be thwarted when they remembered Canada was in the way. It became even harder when many Canadian municipalities declared themselves to be nuclear free zones. Can you imagine how hard it would have been for Gorbachev to explain to the Supreme Soviet that the missile he aimed at Seattle was repelled by the nuclear free zone in Vancouver?

Speaking about Canadian military strengths, few Americans know much about the War of 1812, or, as I like to call it, that time we whooped their butts so badly they have been afraid to fight us ever since. An American colleague of mine called me at home on November 11th a couple of years ago. I told him I wasn't working that day because of the holiday.

"Veteran's Day?" he asked.

"No," I replied, seizing the opportunity to promote Canada's military prowess over his country. "Today is the anniversary of our victory at Chrysler's Farm in 1813 when a vastly outnumbered Canadian force of a few hundred farmers opened up a big old can of whoop-ass on invading Americans. If that hadn't happened I'd be an American."

"Well," he said, "I'm sure neither of us would want that."

In typical Canadian fashion I politely thanked him, even though I was pretty sure he meant that as an insult.

Americans often refer to their leader as the most powerful man in the world. Sure, George Bush could pick up a telephone and single-handedly blow the planet back to the Stone Age. You have to remember though, wherever the American President goes, a small army of Secret Service agents who have been trained to jump in front of a bullet surrounds him. With that kind of back-up Richard Simmons could call himself the most powerful man in the world.

When Jean Chrétien was our Prime Minister, he proved he could take pretty good care of himself. I'm proud of the fact my leader had the resourcefulness to arm himself with an Inuit carving while his wife slammed the bedroom door on a knife-wielding intruder. OK, so no one would ever make it that far into the living quarters at the White House, but at least Chrétien was ready when his guards let him down.

So yes, Canada, in my own way I stand on guard for thee when I am in the United States. I ask for directions to the washroom at a gas station, not the restroom or the bathroom because I don't go there for a rest or a bath, but I do plan on washing. I order pop with my hamburger, not a soda. I am proud to be from the country that sent them John Candy and Mike Myers, Bryan Adams and Neil Young, Wayne Gretzky and Larry Walker, even if they think of those stars as Americans. I'm glad that it was a Canadian newspaper that gave Ernest Hemmingway his start. I'm even happier one gave me mine.

I am Canadian all right. (I just hope the Americans are OK with that, because, after all we're supposed to be polite and I wouldn't want to offend them, eh?)

About The Author

Gordon Kirkland was born in Toronto, Ontario, Canada in 1953. He met his wife, Diane, while still in high school in London, Ontario. Married in 1973, they've spent over thirty years as each other's best friend. They have two grown sons, Mike and Brad.

Since 1982, they've lived on Canada's West Coast in a small semi-rural community near Vancouver, British Columbia.

Gordon became partially paralyzed in a 1990 automobile accident. He jokes that it was really a golfing accident, because he was on his way to play golf when his car was rear-ended. In 1992, he was once again hit from behind by an errant driver. When it happened again in 1994, this time by a member of the Royal Canadian Mounted Police, he began to think even numbered years in the 1990's were out to get him.

He was almost afraid to drive in 1996.

He spent his working life writing in a variety of functions ranging from public relations and advertising to marketing and strategic planning. Immediately prior to his first accident, he wrote six books for the Government of Canada focusing on trade opportunities in countries in Southeast Asia.

Diane encouraged him to start writing the way he would like to, rather than writing what other people wanted him to write for them. He chose to focus on humor, partially because of his upbringing in a family that included a great deal of laughter, and because, during his hospital rehabilitation after the accidents, he learned laughter causes the body to produce endorphins that are ten times stronger than morphine.

As he says, "...and I was so enjoying the morphine."

The result has been his four previous books and the book you are now holding.

His first, Justice *Is Blind - And Her Dog Just Peed In My Cornflakes*, won Canada's Stephen Leacock Award of Merit for Humour in 2000. His second, *Never Stand Behind A Loaded Horse*, won the same award in 2005. Following the trend, his third book, *When My Mind Wanders It Brings Back Souvenirs*, won him his third Award of Merit in 2006 . At this writing, we are waiting to hear what awards his fourth book, *I Think I'm Having One Of Those Decades*, might receive.

In addition to his books, his weekly syndicated humor column, *Gordon Kirkland At Large*, has appeared in Canadian and American newspapers since August, 1994. In that time he has written hundreds of newspaper columns and feature articles, a live comedy CD, a live audio book, and four volumes of contact management information for writers.

Gordon's life and humor have been profiled in magazines and newspapers throughout North America, including a feature article in the April 2006 issue of the Canadian edition of Reader's Digest. He has appeared on dozens of radio and television talk shows, as well performing his material as in theaters and comedy venues.

Each year, he makes himself available to writer's conferences, festivals and workshops, where he teaches a wide variety of topics ranging from humor writing to book marketing. Most notably, he has twice been named to the faculty of the prestigious *Erma Bombeck Writers' Workshop* at the University of Dayton in Ohio.

His outlook on life, which shines through in his writing, makes him living proof that adversity and life's difficult events can be handled successfully as long as you maintain your sense of humor.

About The Caricature Logo

The caricature seen above has been used as Gordon Kirkland's logo on documents and on the gordonkirkland.com website for the past several years. This is the first time it is being used as part of a book cover. It was created by editorial cartoonist Milt Priggee (www.miltpriggee.com).

Beginning in 1978, he was the regular cartoonist for the weekly Crain's Chicago Business. The Journal Herald in Dayton, Ohio hired Priggee in July of 1982. When the Journal Herald ceased publication in 1986, he landed at The Spokesman-Review in Spokane, Washington, in February 1987. His work has been reprinted in Time, Newsweek, U.S. News & World Report, The New York Times, Washington Post, USA Today, and CNN's Headline News. He has been an award winner in the Associated Press Society of Ohio, Mencken Awards, National Newspaper Association, Overseas Press Club, the Small Business Foundation of America, Inc., Pacific

Northwest Journalists, the Fischetti Editorial Cartoon, and The First Iran Internet Cartoon contests.

From 2000-2001, Milt attended the University of Michigan on a Journalism Fellowship. Currently he is self-syndicated from his base in Oak Harbor, WA, where he continues to produce cartoons on local, national, and world topics.

Printed in the United States
106691LV00003B/343-360/A